Estranged Friends?
The Transatlantic
Consequences
of Societal Change

Estranged Friends?
The Transatlantic
Consequences
of Societal Change

Max Kaase

and

Andrew Kohut

COUNCIL ON FOREIGN RELATIONS PRESS

NEW YORK

The Council on Foreign Relations, Inc., is a nonprofit and nonpartisan organization devoted to promoting improved understanding of international affairs through the free exchange of ideas. The Council does not take any position on questions of foreign policy and has no affiliation with, and receives no funding from, the United States government.

If you would like more information on Council publications, please write the Council on Foreign Relations, 58 East 68th Street, New York, NY 10021, or call the Publications Office at (212) 734-0400.

Copyright © 1996 by the Bertelsmann Foundation Publishers.
All rights reserved.
Printed in the United States of America.

This book may not be reproduced, in whole or in part, in any form (beyond that copying permitted by Sections 107 and 108 of the U.S. Copyright Law and excerpts by reviewers for the public press), without written permission from the publishers. For information, write Publications Office, Council on Foreign Relations, 58 East 68th Street, New York, NY 10021.

Library of Congress Cataloging-in-Publication Data

Kaase, Max.
   Estranged Friends? : The Transatlantic Consequences of Societal
Change / by Max Kaase and Andrew Kohut.
      p.   cm.
   Inclsudes bibliographical references and index.
   ISBN 0-87609-185-0
      1. United States—Foreign relations—1989—Public opinion.
   2. United States—Foreign relations—Europe—Public opinion.
   3. Europe—Foreign relations—United States—Public opinion.
   4. Social change—United States.
   5. Public opinion—United States.
      6. United States—Social conditions—1980.   7. United States—Politics and government—government—1989.   8.   Political   Participation—United   States.   I. Kohut,
Andrew.   II. Title
   E840.K28   1995
   327.73—dc20
                                                          95-45169
                                                             CIP

96   97   98   PB   10   9   8   7   6   5   4   3   2   1

Cover Design: Dorothy Wachtenheim

Contents

Societal Change in the United States and Its Transatlantic Consequences from an Empirical Perspective
Andrew Kohut

Foreword

The transatlantic partnership now finds itself at the beginning of a series of challenges and tests of its stability and reliability. After a long period of security and certainty, the United States and Europe have unexpectedly been confronted with a bewildering array of problems that require joint strategies and responses and a redefinition of their partnership.

Europe is in the middle of a historic process in which the framework and the factors that determine foreign policy, as well as the foreign policies themselves, are subject to fundamental change. The task facing a united Germany is to find a meaningful and pragmatic way through the unusually complicated maze of historical preconditions and contemporary challenges that demonstrates responsibility, historically based caution, and a commitment to an involved foreign policy.

Similarly, the United States is currently in search of a new role in a changed international environment. The new majority in Congress has, if anything, made the foreign policy decision-making process even more difficult. Caught between an inward-looking tendency and its status as the leading world power, the United States is faced with the problem of finding a specific role in relation to its partners, both within the western alliance and with regard to the rest of the world, particularly those states whose hopes and expectations are pinned on gaining admittance to the western and transatlantic communities.

The following two studies examine the fundamental foreign policy attitudes of both ordinary citizens and elites. In his essay,

Max Kaase provides a thorough and precise analysis of the basic social preconditions that underlie the formulation and establishment of a new foreign policy. He comes to the conclusion that the transatlantic alliance, even after the East-West confrontation, enjoys a high level of popular support. Nevertheless, two tendencies illustrate some of the problems that confront the new epoch:

- In general terms the change in values is lowering the status of security policy and changing public opinion, which may thus shift toward transatlantic indifference or distance.

- The public opinion leadership of the elites can redress the balance, though only on the basis of a new discursive justification for the alliance's raison d'être.

Foreign policy attitudes are characterized on the one hand by candor, participation, and the willingness to engage in discourse, and on the other by criticism of the European Union and adherence to a policy of abstinence and restraint.

On the basis of representative surveys, Andrew Kohut provides a detailed and comprehensive description of the attitudes and values of American citizens and elites with regard to the global role of the United States. From this, the study deduces the foreign policy roles and tasks that are most likely to receive support from the American people in the new era.

Public opinion in the United States is characterized by a greater interest in domestic problems, by the subsuming of foreign policy problems to economic viewpoints, and by the differences between the elites and the rest of the population that derive from the fact that the majority of U.S. citizens tend to be more interested in domestic policy. Kohut's study describes American attitudes toward foreign policy and their value-based origins, and suggests potential ways of dealing with them in the future.

Established common interests continue to form a link between the transatlantic partners. The structures that helped to overcome the Cold War and successfully prevent the outbreak of an open conflict still survive and continue to function. Furthermore, the attitudes of citizens and elites on both sides of the Atlantic are capable of forming a solid foundation of partnership and responsibility on which it is possible to establish a common foreign policy. Yet as Kohut and Kaase so impressively demonstrate, there is some cause for concern. The authors describe the necessity for future transatlantic coordination and action. Indeed, intensive consultation and cooperation are now needed more than they have ever been; without them, there is a risk that the mature partnership will degenerate into narcissism and relapse to the level of national selfishness.

Both studies were written in the context of a joint project on the future of the transatlantic relationship, a collaborative effort by the Council on Foreign Relations, the Research Group on European Affairs at the University of Munich, and the Bertelsmann Foundation. We would like to extend our special thanks to Sonja Niedermaier and Susan Scott for their work on editing and producing this book.

Leslie H. Gelb
President of the Council
on Foreign Relations,
New York

Werner Weidenfeld
Member of the Board of
the Bertelsmann Foundation;
Director of the Research Group
on European Affairs,
University of Munich

The Impact of Sociopolitical Change in Western Europe on Transatlantic Relations

Max Kaase

1. INTRODUCTION

In the second half of the twentieth century, the people of Western Europe and the United States have experienced a period of unprecedented economic well-being and growth. The breakdown of formerly democratic states like Germany and Italy in the 1920s and 1930s, as well as the emergence of the Soviet Union as a totalitarian world power, along with the extension of its sphere of influence into Central and Eastern Europe, had been developments with a deep impact on political thinking in the West after the war. They all contributed to the conviction—especially among political elites, but also among many citizens in Western democracies—that democracy was the answer to the challenging question of the optimal organization of the modern state.

The downfall of the Weimar Republic served as an example of the important role economic stability and growth play in the public's acceptance of democratic political institutions and procedures. It is now widely agreed that the unique combination of market economy and liberal, representative democracy and—in Western Europe—of some variant of the welfare state has been a decisive factor in democracy's triumph in the great ideological confrontation of the Cold War between democracy and communism.

A wealth of objective indicators testifies amply to the enormous economic growth that the United States and West European states have in varying degrees experienced since the 1950s. (See, for example, the growth in the number of automobiles according to figure 1; furthermore, see

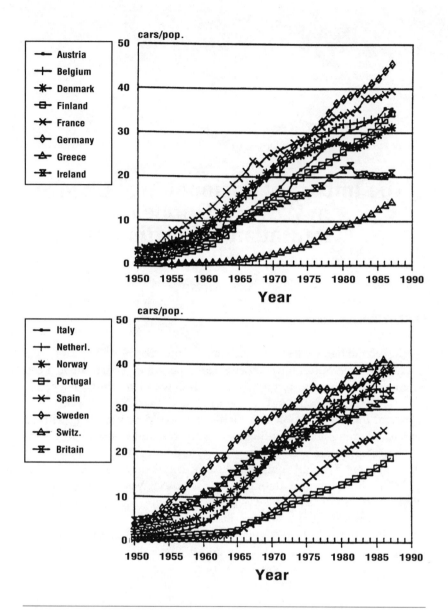

FIGURE 1. DISTRIBUTION OF CARS IN WESTERN EUROPE 1950–87
(NUMBER OF CARS PER 100 INHABITANTS)

Source: U.N. Statistical Yearbooks, as published in Jan W. van Deth, "A Macro-Setting for Micro-Politics," in Jan W. van Deth and Elinor Scarbrough, eds., *The Impact of Values* (Oxford: Oxford University Press, 1995).

tables 1 and 2.) As one consequence, full employment, especially in the 1960s, for most countries was almost to be taken for granted; even in countries where the situation was not quite so positive, this was scarcely a problem (see table 3). One of the most important aspects of economic growth was the change in sectoral employment. Between 1970 and 1980 most of the Organization for Economic Cooperation and Development (OECD) countries had completed their transition to what in the 1970s

TABLE 1.   REAL GDP PER CAPITA IN INTERNATIONAL PRICES
(CONSTANT PRICES; US $ AT 1980 EXCHANGE RATE) 1950–85

	1950	1960	1970	1980	1985
Aus.	2,318	3,908	5,843	8,230	8,929
Belg.	3,462	4,379	6,750	9,228	9,717
Den.	4,241	5,490	7,776	9,598	10,884
Fin.	2,758	4,073	6,186	8,393	9,232
Fr.	3,125	4,473	7,078	9,688	9,918
FRG	2,713	5,217	7,443	9,795	10,708
Gr.	986	1,474	2,952	4,383	4,464
Ice.	3,592	4,644	6,157	9,285	9,037
Ire.	2,047	2,545	3,628	4,929	5,205
It.	1,929	3,233	5,028	7,164	7,425
Lux.	5,286	6,112	7,857	10,173	10,540
Neth.	3,404	4,690	6,915	9,036	9,092
Norw.	3,802	5,001	7,104	11,094	12,623
Port.	937	1,429	2,575	3,733	3,729
Sp.	1,640	2,425	4,379	6,131	6,437
Sw.	3,980	5,149	7,401	8,863	9,904
Switz.	4,886	6,834	9,164	10,013	10,640
Turk.	822	1,255	1,702	2,319	2,533
UK	3,993	4,970	6,319	7,975	8,665
Can.	5,337	6,069	8,495	11,332	12,196
USA	6,401	7,380	9,459	11,404	12,532
Jap.	1,129	2,239	5,496	8,117	9,447
Austral.	4,331	5,182	7,344	8,349	8,850
NZ	4,531	5,571	6,595	7,363	8,000

Source: Jan-Erik Lane, David McKay, and Kenneth Newton, *Political Data Handbook: OECD Countries* (New York: Oxford University Press, 1991), p. 49.
Note: Real GDP per capita is adjusted for differences in the purchasing power of currencies, that is, efforts have been made to make better international comparisons.

TABLE 2.   GROWTH OF REAL GDP
(YEAR-TO-YEAR AVERAGES) 1950–81

	1950–60	1960–70	1970–81
Aus.	5.9	4.6	3.5
Belg.	2.7[a]	4.7	3.0
Den.	3.2	4.7	2.1
Fin.	4.4	4.3	3.1
Fr.	4.4	5.5	3.3
FRG	7.7	4.4	2.6
Gr.	6.0	7.5	4.3
Ice.	5.5	4.5	4.3
Ire.	1.3	4.2	4.0
It.	5.5[b]	5.7	2.9
Lux.	2.7[c]	3.4	2.4
Neth.	4.6	5.3	2.7
Norw.	3.6	4.9	4.5
Port.	4.1	5.9	4.2
Sp.	3.6[d]	7.1	3.4
Sw.	3.6	4.4	1.8
Switz.	4.2	4.3	0.7
Turk.	6.3	6.0	5.2
UK	2.7	2.9	1.7
Can.	4.0	5.6	3.8
USA	2.9	4.4	2.9
Jap.	8.0[e]	10.4	4.5
Austral.	4.3[a]	5.9	2.8
NZ	2.4	3.7	2.0

Source: Lane, McKay, and Newton, Political Data Handbook, p. 61.
[a]1953–60.
[b]1951–60.
[c]1950–59.
[d]1954–60.
[e]1952–60.

Daniel Bell called postindustrial societies, with more than 50 percent of those economically active employed in the service sector (see table 4).[1]

In the context of this study, two corollaries of these developments are particularly relevant. The first is the pervasive rise of secondary education (see figure 2), and the second is the advent of television as a new medium of electronic communication (see figure 3).

TABLE 3. UNEMPLOYED WORKERS AS A PERCENTAGE OF TOTAL
LABOR FORCE 1960–85

	1960	1970	1975	1980	1985
Aus.	2.4	1.4	1.7	1.6	4.1
Belg.	3.3	1.8	4.4	7.7	12.0
Den.ᵃ	1.9	0.7	4.9	6.5	7.3
Fin.	1.4	1.9	2.2	4.6	4.8
Fr.	1.2	2.4	4.1	6.3	10.2
FRG	1.0	0.6	4.0	3.3	8.3
Gr.ᵃ	6.1	4.2	2.3	2.8	7.8
Ice.ᵃ	—	1.2	1.1	1.0	0.9
Ire.ᵃ	5.6	5.8	7.3	7.3	17.4
It.	5.5	5.3	5.8	7.5	9.9
Lux.ᵃ	—	0.7	0.6	0.6	1.9
Neth.	0.7	1.0	5.2	6.0	12.8
Norw.	1.2	1.6	2.3	1.7	2.5
Port.ᵃ	1.9	2.5	4.4	7.7	9.0
Sp.	2.3	2.5	4.3	12.3	21.5
Sw.	1.7	1.5	1.6	2.0	2.8
Switz.	—	0.0	0.3	0.2	0.9
Turk.ᵃ	9.2	12.0	12.9	14.4	15.9
UK	1.3	2.2	3.2	5.6	11.5
Can.	6.4	5.6	6.9	7.4	10.4
USA	5.3	4.8	8.3	7.0	7.1
Jap.	1.7	1.1	1.9	2.0	2.6
Austral.	1.4	1.6	4.8	6.0	8.2
NZᵃ	0.1	0.2	0.2	2.2	4.1

Source: Lane, McKay, and Newton, *Political Data Handbook*, p. 41.
ᵃDenotes a different national definition of unemployment, whereas other countries adhere
to OECD standards.

The combined effects of these changes in the economic and socio-structural makeup of the societies under scrutiny on the political orientations of the citizenry will be central to the following analysis. Obviously, in principle, such a wide array of topics and issues is eligible for further consideration, so that some enlightened decision had to be taken regarding the fields on which this study should concentrate. Given the overar-

TABLE 4. SERVICE WORKERS AS A PERCENTAGE OF
ECONOMICALLY ACTIVE POPULATION IN CIVILIAN EMPLOYMENT

	International Labor Organization figures				Organization for Economic Cooperation and Development figures			
	1950	1960	1970	1980	1960	1970	1980	1985
Aus.	30.8	36.2	44.4	50.5	35.7	43.2	51.4	55.3
Belg.	39.2	45.5	51.9	62.9	46.4	53.2	62.9	67.4
Den.	41.6	45.9	51.7	61.9	44.8	50.7	62.4	65.2
Fin.	26.3	33.1	45.5	54.2	32.2	42.8	51.8	56.5
Fr.	35.4	41.6	43.9	55.3	38.5	47.2	55.4	60.4
FRG	36.4	39.3	44.6	49.5	39.1	42.9	50.3	53.5
Gr.	32.5	25.0	33.0	41.9	25.5	34.2	39.5	43.8
Ice.	32.4	43.3	44.0	49.0	42.4	44.6	49.8	52.7
Ire.	36.1	39.4	43.2	49.4	39.0	43.1	49.2	55.1
It.	25.7	30.6	36.6	49.4	33.5	40.3	47.8	55.2
Lux.	34.5	42.0	58.1	62.4	38.4	46.8	56.5	62.3
Neth.	43.8	48.0	57.3	64.0	49.7	54.9	63.6	68.6
Norw.	37.7	44.0	51.1	62.6	42.9	48.8	61.8	65.0
Port.	26.7	28.3	38.8	41.9	24.8	37.1	36.1	41.5
Sp.	25.0	30.1	37.7	48.4	31.0	37.4	45.1	50.6
Sw.	42.7	41.1	52.4	62.3	44.0	53.5	62.2	65.3
Switz.	37.0	38.3	43.9	54.8	38.9	45.5	53.4	55.7
Turk.	7.4	15.3	20.1	25.5	10.7	14.5	23.1	25.4
UK	45.9	48.9	59.2	59.2	47.6	52.0	59.7	65.1
Can.	45.4	54.7	61.3	66.7	54.1	61.4	66.0	69.3
USA	53.5	58.4	61.9	66.2	56.2	61.1	65.9	68.8
Jap.	29.1	37.7	46.2	54.9	41.3	46.9	54.2	56.4
Austral.	46.0	49.9	58.4	66.5	50.1	55.0	62.4	66.2
NZ	50.6	48.9	53.3	57.9	46.8	48.6	55.4	56.5

Source: Lane, McKay, and Newton, *Political Data Handbook,* p. 36.
Note: Service workers are those employed in wholesale and retail trade, restaurants and
hotels, transport, storage and communication, financing, insurance, real estate and
business systems, community and social and personal services, and related services.

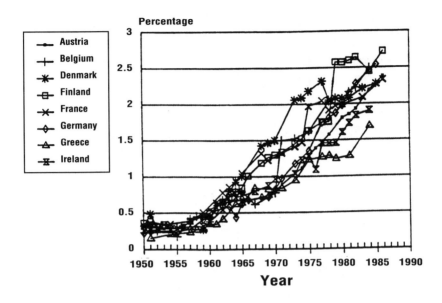

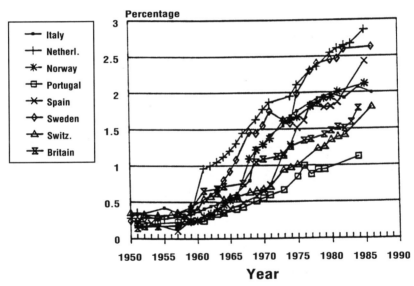

FIGURE 2.   STUDENT PARTICIPATION IN HIGHER EDUCATION IN
WESTERN EUROPE 1950–86 (PERCENTAGE OF TOTAL POPULATION)

Sources: U.N. Statistical Yearbooks. Figure taken from van Deth (1995).

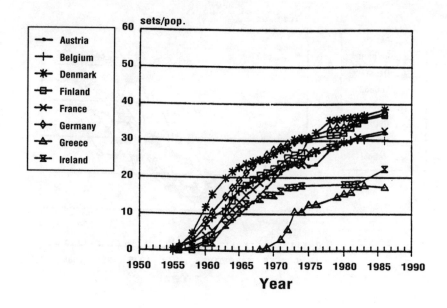

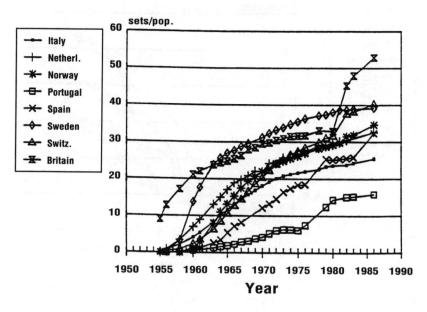

FIGURE 3.   DISTRIBUTION OF TELEVISION SETS IN WESTERN EUROPE 1950–86
(NUMBER OF SETS PER 100 INHABITANTS)

Sources: U.N. Statistical Yearbooks. Figure taken from van Deth (1995).

ching theme of the future of relations between Europe and the United States, it must also be borne in mind that the direction, quality, and content of this relationship are to a large, though probably shrinking, extent a matter of elite action and elite decision-making.

Public opinion research, predominantly based on random samples of the voting-age population, has over the years created a wealth of reliable information on the political beliefs of the citizenry. However, systematic and longitudinal comparative studies of elite orientations or even cross-sectional studies comparing elites and nonelites are close to nonexistent. Therefore, the data on the United States presented by Andrew Kohut in this volume, contrasting elites and nonelites, is an extremely welcome addition.

The scarcity of knowledge on elite orientations is not the only reason why the following discussion concentrates on presenting public opinion research data from representative sample surveys. As will soon become apparent, structural developments already briefly alluded to have resulted in what some social scientists have come to term the "participatory revolution." The widening political repertory of the electorate, especially among the young and educated, has become a common feature of all Western democracies and has rendered previously quite distinct boundaries between elites and mass publics more fuzzy. In addition, the omnipresence of television cameras has opened up for groups such as the new social movements—a summary term for groups emphasizing issues such as peace, the environment, and gender equality—fresh avenues of access to political decision-makers beyond traditional institutionalized channels. It is thus worthwhile to take a detailed look at how the political orientations of mass publics in Western Europe have unfolded over the last 20 to 30 years.

In order to provide conceptual coherence in this report, it is useful to follow a heuristic strategy that has emerged over many years of research in the description and explanation of citizens' political attitudes and behavior. This strategy is graphically represented in the following diagram.

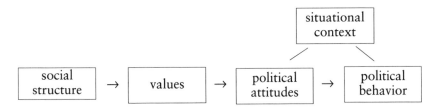

The causal relationship between these dimensions, especially from a dynamic, longitudinal perspective, is far from unidirectional and simplistic. These complexities cannot be dealt with here. Rather, the task of the following analyses is to give some reliable information as the basis on which transatlantic relations can be further developed. Through an analysis of the broad changes occurring in Western publics, a better sense can be gained of constraints and opportunities in this regard.

Finally for this introductory section, although admittedly highly speculative, the question should at least be raised of whether the decline of communism, the increasing importance of transnational issues (for example, migration and the environment), apparent structural economic problems (particularly unemployment) in almost all of the OECD countries, and the rise in crime and violence in these countries do not mark the end of a historical epoch of continuing economic growth and well-being, as well as of a high level of societal peace.

The ongoing debate in the West on the concept of "civil society" may well highlight the fact that, with the strains just mentioned, the question of the principal political organization of modern democratic societies is once again gaining attention. While Western core notions of the market and liberal constitutional democracy still seem to be the only ones that have successfully survived the twentieth-century competition of ideas related to the structuring of society and polity, these ideas are but means to undefined ends; they are, to use a phrase coined by Ralf Dahrendorf, "cold projects." Such an observation can easily be related to concepts such as individualization, postmodernism, deconstructionism, hedonism, and secularization, all of which figure prominently in contemporary cultural and social science discourse. These worldviews point to the loss of an integrating ideational fabric in contemporary Western societies.[2]

At first sight, such concerns may not appear to be of immediate relevance to transatlantic cooperation. On closer inspection, however, they will reveal that the domestic context and basis of this cooperation have become increasingly dependent on a broad variety of factors besides elite consensus.

2. SOME METHODOLOGICAL CONSIDERATIONS AND THE DATA BASE

The analysis of change is a classic theme for the social sciences. While census data and other processed-produced statistical information have been used for a long time to measure the "objective" state of societal and, especially, economic affairs, this is not equally true of micro-level data dealing with the attitudes and behavior of individual members of a given society. It was the special combination of statistical procedures to design probability samples, together with the development since the 1940s of a methodology able to validly and reliably measure individual properties, that led to the flourishing field known today as survey or public opinion research. There is no question that these domains are now fully established as a standard element in the self-observation of modern societies. Because this source of information will have existed for about 50 years by the turn of the century, public opinion surveys will also increasingly become part of standard empirical procedures used in historical research.

Anyone interested in this particular longitudinal feature of survey research (which is mandatory for the analysis of sociopolitical change) will soon encounter a series of caveats. To start with, the monitoring of individual orientations across time, as practiced in panel research, confronts specific methodological and empirical difficulties. This problem is raised here briefly in order to emphasize that for the time being, the best that broadly oriented research on sociopolitical change can hope for is a series of independent cross-sectional surveys along the time dimension.

There is no point in dwelling on the pitfalls even of this more limited approach to the study of change, such as the comparability of sampling designs and consistency in question wording as necessary (though not sufficient) conditions for this type of research. What is much more important is that of the tens of thousands of survey studies conducted every year around the globe, the vast majority do not explicitly consider the time dimension. As a result, there is much less continuity in survey research than one might have hoped.

While there is at least a certain amount of written documentation on longitudinal results from survey research, for the social researcher it is much more important to obtain direct access to data sources in order to conduct proper secondary research.[3] Over the last 30 years in many OECD countries survey data archives have been established that provide access to original data from studies conducted in the past. These data sets, however, frequently come from academic scholars. As a result, relatively few of them emphasize a wide variety of topics as well as theoretical perspectives. Longitudinal studies, prominent in electoral sociology, and the general social surveys conducted in many of the OECD countries are the exception rather than the rule. Privately funded survey studies are usually monopolized by the commissioning party or survey research institute conducting the study. In short, the potential for longitudinal research is rather limited. This situation contrasts sharply with the growing emphasis placed in the social sciences on the time dimension.

A further complication arises when one wishes to transcend the limits of one's own nation to look for cross-sectional as well as longitudinal *comparative* survey research evidence. This is, of course, exactly the type of evidence required to deal properly with the topic of this study. Cross-national survey research is extremely rare, and even rarer in longitudinal terms. For Western Europe, the most pertinent database is represented by the so-called Eurobarometer studies, which are cross-sectional comparative surveys conducted biannually in the member countries of the European Union on behalf of the European Commission. An important advantage of the Eurobarometers is that they started as early as 1974, have maintained a limited, but largely consistent, set of questions, and are therefore ideally suited to longitudinal analysis. Their major weakness is that owing to the relatively small resources the Eurobarometer program commands, the number of questions regularly asked is quite small and, understandably, many of these questions deal with attitudes toward Europe and the EU.

Fortunately, a research program entitled "Beliefs in Government," funded by the European Science Foundation in Strasbourg since 1989, and jointly directed by Professor Kenneth Newton of the University of Essex in Colchester and this author, has recently been completed in 1994. It deals with the evolution of citizen orientations vis-à-vis various dimensions of politics in Western Europe since the 1960s. This program has been based exclusively on available secondary data and therefore provides an almost complete overview of the existing databases. Many of the findings presented in this study are based on this project.

3. THE FABRIC OF SOCIOPOLITICAL CHANGE

On the one hand, speculations both before and after the Second World War asserted that modern states would be on the road to mass society, the latter being conceptualized—for example, by William Kornhauser—as a breakdown of the system of institutions and organizations mediating between the state and the individual.[4] On the other hand, the well-known dictum of Lipset and Rokkan that European party systems of the 1960s reflected the cleavages and constitutive sociopolitical conflicts of the 1920s was derived from the observation of a surprising amount of stability in European intermediary structures, as far as political parties were concerned.

Some of these speculations were not buttressed by empirical evidence at all. Other analyses reflected a state of affairs that was still characterized widely by the regained political stability of the 1950s and early 1960s. Thus the passage of time, the availability of at least some longitudinal empirical evidence, and other problems necessitate a fresh look at the validity of such perceptions of ongoing changes in modern societies.

Regarding the party systems in the West, the evidence is still strong that much less change has been taking place than one might have anticipated, given enormous upheavals in the overall social structure of the societies in question.[5] Nevertheless, there can be no question that substantial rearrangements of the relationships between citizens and political parties have taken place over the last 20 years. In this respect, three developments deserve special mention.

The first is the rise of various Green parties in Western Europe.[6] When this development began in the early 1980s, many observers expected— given the precarious voter base and many institutional hurdles (in Germany the five percent clause banning all parties with less than five percent of the second ballot from access to parliament)—that the Greens would turn out to be an ephemeral phenomenon. After more than a decade of Green parties, however, this expectation has not been borne out. Rather, in almost all West European polities, Green parties and politics (particularly on the subnational level) have become an integral part of political normality. Analyses abound relating "Greenism" to the rise of postmaterialism, which began in the late 1960s.[7]

The second development regarding political parties is the increased volatility of voters, as the established cleavages, social milieus, and related elite networks that had stabilized voter-party relationships for a long time—indeed until the 1960s—began to wane.[8] The rise of issue politics is one topic of scholarly discourse under this conceptual heading.

Third, leaving open the tricky question of cause and effect, there can be no question that—as in the United States in the 1960s—in most West European democracies both identification with political parties and strength of party identification have been undergoing a process of slow but consistent erosion that has certainly contributed to increased voter volatility (see table 5). It is an open question to what extent such processes

TABLE 5. EVOLUTION OF PARTISANSHIP ACROSS TIME IN 14 WEST EUROPEAN COUNTRIES AND THE UNITED STATES: RESULTS OF LINEAR REGRESSION ANALYSIS USING NATIONAL ELECTION STUDIES AND EUROBAROMETER DATA

Country	Data source	Period covered	Number of observations	Strong identifiers		All identifiers	
				Intercept	b-values	Intercept	b-values
USA	NES	1952–92	11	36.7	−0.25*	78.4	−0.44**
Ireland	EB	1978–92	15	35.6	−0.96**	61.8	−1.83**
Italy	EB	1978–92	15	45.8	−1.00**	78.6	−1.50**
France	EB	1975–92	18	26.9	−0.60*	66.9	−0.86**
Britain	NES	1964–92	9	46.0	−1.21**	92.0	−0.78**
	EB	1978–92	15	33.4	0.02	60.5	−0.81*
Sweden	NES	1956–91	12	48.6	−0.65**	—	
	NES	1968–91	9	38.0	−0.49*	66.1	−0.70**
Luxembourg	EB	1975–92	18	28.5	−0.56**	61.9	−0.74*
Germany	NES	1961–90	9		—	38.6	0.26
	NES	1972–90	6	16.1	−0.38	52.8	−0.66
	EB	1975–92	18	33.2	−0.26	69.8	−0.52
Netherlands	NES	1971–89	6	22.4	−0.01	38.9	−0.11
	EB	1975–92	18	36.3	−0.42*	75.7	0.09
Norway	NES	1965–89	7	36.9	−0.08	66.9	−0.04
Denmark	NES	1971–89	7	28.9	−0.07	50.3	0.07
	EB	1976–92	17	36.7	−0.37*	67.4	0.01

Belgium	EB	1975–92	18	25.7	-0.37	50.8	-0.10
Portugal	EB	1985–92	8	14.8	-0.62	60.3	0.18
Greece	EB	1981–92	12	35.6	-0.17	63.0	0.52
Spain	EB	1985–92	8	10.5	0.37*	35.9	0.81
EC-9	EB	1978–92	15	35.6	-0.47*	71.2	-0.89**

Source: Hermann Schmitt and Sören Holmberg, "Political Parties in Decline?," in H.-D. Klingemann and D. Fuchs, eds., *Citizens and the State,* Beliefs in Government Series, vol. 1 (Oxford: Oxford University Press, 1995), pp. 95–133.

Notes: —— signifies "not available"; data could not be estimated because of changes in question wording. Country-specific ordinary least squares regressions were performed with proportion of party identifiers as the dependent variable and year as the independent variable. Number of observations means number of elections in the case of NES, and number of years covered in Eurobarometers. For NES, the number of elections is not equivalent to the number of surveys; in some cases, more than one survey contained the party identification measure, and the findings are averaged; in other instances (e.g., in Denmark), some election studies did not include the party identification measure. EC9 is the "old" European Community of nine member-countries (Belgium, Denmark, France, Germany, Great Britain, Ireland, Italy, Luxembourg, and the Netherlands); for these countries, equivalent Eurobarometer data are available from 1978 on; pooled analyses are run on the basis of weighted data with national sample sizes adjusted to the relative population weight within the Community. We used the Irish "closely attached" to exemplify how to read these figures. In 1978 strong party identifiers comprised 35.6 percent of the adult population; this level has been declining by approximately 1 percent per year since then (precisely, –0.96 percent) and approached the 20 percent mark in 1992 (35.6 + (15* –0.96)).

*Significant at the 0.05 level. **Significant at the 0.005 level. Two-tailed *t*-tests were applied.

within multiparty systems will result in mounting difficulties in creating governments, in growing governmental instability within a parliamentary period, and in decreasing possibilities of finding sufficient consensus among the electorate for critical political decision-making.

Beyond weakening bonds between voters and parties, it has been claimed in recent discussions that parties are also beginning to lose ground as intermediary organizations in other ways—for instance, in recruiting qualified personnel for political posts. These are questions for which reliable cross-national evidence is hardly available.[9] At least in one respect—namely, party membership—a gloomy view of the future of political parties seems not to be warranted. There is, however, some evidence that, in addition to the usual medium-range fluctuations in membership strength, in Denmark, Finland, and Great Britain, a long-term trend toward a decrease in the number of party members exists. (This information is based on party records; see table 6 for details.)

Next to political parties, trade unions are traditionally regarded as the most important intermediary corporate actors in modern democracies. Here, too, speculation abounds regarding their waning strength as a result of the changing structure of the economy and employment on the one hand, and of decreasing trade union membership on the other. Nevertheless, the available evidence contradicts at least the latter notion (see table 7). For the 1950–1985 period, little empirical support can be mustered for the claim that trade unions are losing membership on a large scale.

Obviously, intermediation is not confined to parties and trade unions. For lack of additional data, nothing can be said here about the many other intermediary organizations integrating an individual into the fabric of a given society. There are, however, two additional aspects of intermediation that need to be addressed at this point. The first relates to the advent of television and other modern electronic media of communication. Undoubtedly, citizens in contemporary societies are integrated into the social process increasingly in an indirect, virtual manner, too. This holds especially true for politics, about which people get by far the most information through the media. It remains an open question how this fact influences people's thinking on political matters and whether and how it impinges on their view of the world. It is clear, however, that the mass media have become important competitors for organizational membership in the intermediation process.

TABLE 6. PARTY MEMBERSHIP IN TEN WEST EUROPEAN COUNTRIES 1960–89: PARTY RECORDS

	BE	DK	FI	GE	IR	IT	NL	NO	SV	GB
1960	—	21	—	—	—	—	—	—	10	—
1961	8	—	—	3	—	—	—	16	—	—
1962	—	—	19	—	—	—	—	—	—	—
1963	—	—	—	—	—	13	9	—	—	10
1964	—	19	—	—	—	—	—	—	10	9
1965	7	—	—	3	—	—	—	16	—	—
1966	—	17	19	—	—	—	—	—	—	9
1967	—	—	—	—	—	—	6	—	—	—
1968	8	16	—	—	—	12	—	—	8	—
1969	—	—	—	3	—	—	—	15	—	—
1970	—	—	17	—	—	—	—	—	8	8
1971	8	14	—	—	—	—	4	—	—	—
1972	—	—	17	4	—	13	4	—	—	—
1973	—	11	—	—	—	—	—	13	8	—
1974	9	—	—	—	—	—	—	—	—	6
1975	—	10	15	—	—	—	—	—	—	—
1976	—	—	—	5	—	10	—	—	8	—
1977	9	8	—	—	1	—	4	14	—	—
1978	9	—	—	—	—	—	—	—	—	—
1979	—	8	15	—	—	10	—	—	8	5
1980	—	—	—	5	—	—	—	—	—	—
1981	9	8	—	—	2	—	4	15	—	—
1982	—	—	—	—	2	—	—	—	8	—
1983	—	—	14	4	—	9	4	—	—	4
1984	—	7	—	—	—	—	—	—	—	—
1985	9	—	—	—	—	—	—	16	8	—
1986	—	—	—	—	—	—	3	—	—	—
1987	9	7	13	4	5	10	—	—	—	3
1988	—	7	—	—	—	—	—	—	8	—
1989	—	—	—	—	5	—	3	13	—	—

Sources: Anders Windfeldt, "Political Parties as Linkage: The Role of the Members," in H.-D. Klingemann and D. Fuchs, eds., Citizens and the State, pp. 134–82; "The Membership in Political Parties in European Democracies: 1960–90," Richard Katz and Peter Mair, eds., European Journal of Political Research, vol. 22, no. 3 (1992); and ———, The Development of Party Organization in Western Democracies: 1966–1990. A Data Handbook (London: Sage, 1992).

Notes: Entries are party members as a percentage of the total electorate, based on membership figures supplied by the parties. The Swedish figures have been adjusted to exclude collectively enrolled members of the Social Democratic Party, assuming an individual membership of 30 percent of the reported total membership.

TABLE 7.   UNION DENSITY RATES IN WESTERN EUROPE

	1950	1960	1970	1980	1985
Denmark	58	63	64	80	82
Norway	50	63	63	63	63
Sweden	68	73	73	88	92
Germany	35	38	38	41	39
Netherlands	43	42	40	35	29
Britain	44	44	49	53	45
France	21	19	21	17	15
Italy	50	35	38	54	51

Source: Kees Aarts, "Linkage and Responsibility: Intermediate Organizations and Interests Representation," in H.-D. Klingemann and Frank D. Fuchs, eds., *Citizens and the State.*
Basis: All wage and salary earners in and out of employment (including retired workers).
Entries: Percentage trade union members.

Precisely because of the linkage function of the mass media, other important actors have emerged. As table 8 shows, the so-called new social movements, despite their fragile and highly subjective membership definition, are now serving as political reference groups for large parts of the citizenry in Western Europe. It appears that they are fulfilling this function in the aggregate in quite a stable fashion (when one examines the percentage of those who, as activists or sympathizers, support the new movements).

At least on the surface, not all movements and their goals appear equally relevant to the transatlantic relationship and the institutions that are the core actors in the context of this relationship. NATO, as the military center of the Western alliance, is certainly confronted with opposition from the peace movement. Of the five countries shown in table 8, West Germany and the Netherlands are where active support for the peace movement is highest. But even in the other three countries the share of potential activists in 1989 amounted to at least ten percent. This is by no means negligible, and it has to be borne in mind that such activists, with respect to skills and resources, are above average in their societies.

TABLE 8.   ATTITUDE TOWARD THREE NEW SOCIAL MOVEMENTS IN FIVE WEST EUROPEAN COUNTRIES 1982–89

Support for the ecology movement (percent).

	France				The Netherlands				West Germany				Italy				Great Britain			
	'82	'84	'86	'89	'82	'84	'86	'89	'82	'84	'86	'89	'82	'84	'86	'89	'82	'84	'86	'89
Activists	0.6	0.3	0.4	1.0	3.2	2.4	2.8	4.4	1.9	0.8	0.7	1.1	0.5	0.9	0.9	0.8	0.4	0.8	1.1	2.7
Potential activists	13.6	11.2	10.1	12.1	25.6	29.5	29.0	40.6	23.9	30.2	26.7	37.9	27.1	19.5	18.0	19.0	19.3	16.3	19.4	28.2
Sympathizers	56.9	66.6	64.9	71.1	54.3	51.5	56.8	47.6	20.6	21.7	25.1	25.7	64.6	69.9	71.9	72.0	47.6	34.5	52.7	53.8
Weak opponents	22.8	18.0	19.5	12.6	11.0	11.8	8.2	6.0	34.9	25.5	29.7	19.7	6.7	7.7	6.6	6.4	24.6	23.6	23.3	12.8
Strong opponents	6.1	3.8	5.0	3.2	5.8	4.7	3.3	1.5	18.7	21.8	17.8	15.6	1.1	1.9	6.6	1.7	8.2	4.9	3.3	2.5
No. of cases	1069	1009	1003	1040	1088	1015	1001	971	1197	992	987	1202	1174	1060	1102	1011	1256	1042	1055	957
Missing cases	24	26	39	12	25	37	24	28	207	149	117	123	91	57	60	28	167	56	116	107

Support for the anti-nuclear power movement (percent).

	France				The Netherlands				West Germany				Italy				Great Britain			
	'82	'84	'86	'89	'82	'84	'86	'89	'82	'84	'86	'89	'82	'84	'86	'89	'82	'84	'86	'89
Activists	0.2	0.3	0.1	0.6	0.8	0.4	0.6	1.6	1.8	0.6	0.6	1.1	0.2	0.9	0.7	0.6	0.4	0.4	1.1	1.8
Potential activists	7.8	4.0	5.1	6.6	14.7	16.2	13.7	18.3	20.7	22.7	23.8	36.3	14.7	10.2	10.2	10.8	19.3	9.5	14.5	13.9
Sympathizers	33.5	38.3	39.1	44.4	40.6	41.5	42.9	47.8	17.9	15.2	17.2	22.0	45.4	48.6	56.0	58.3	30.1	28.3	41.3	36.3
Weak opponents	39.8	42.0	34.8	34.7	19.9	19.2	19.7	20.3	33.5	34.7	32.4	23.5	23.6	28.4	19.0	20.8	26.7	39.4	28.2	31.5
Strong opponents	18.7	15.3	20.9	13.7	24.1	22.7	23.1	11.9	26.1	26.9	25.9	17.1	16.2	12.0	14.2	9.5	23.5	22.0	14.9	16.5
No. of cases	1069	1009	1003	1040	1088	1015	1001	971	1197	992	987	1202	1174	1060	1102	1011	1256	1042	1055	957
Missing cases	34	39	56	34	35	21	14	30	190	165	129	121	134	76	89	45	84	50	56	69

(continued)

TABLE 8. ATTITUDE TOWARD THREE NEW SOCIAL MOVEMENTS IN FIVE WEST EUROPEAN COUNTRIES 1982–89
(continued)

Support for the Peace Movement (percent).

	France				The Netherlands				West Germany				Italy				Great Britain			
	'82	'84	'86	'89	'82	'84	'86	'89	'82	'84	'86	'89	'82	'84	'86	'89	'82	'84	'86	'89
Activists	0.6	0.3	0.1	0.6	1.3	2.2	1.0	1.6	2.4	1.8	1.5	2.7	1.4	1.3	1.2	0.7	1.4	2.1	2.6	2.5
Potential activists	11.7	8.8	9.4	9.4	20.3	21.9	17.7	20.7	36.6	40.5	42.1	45.0	29.0	17.6	17.5	14.8	19.5	11.8	13.8	14.8
Sympathizers	45.4	50.1	48.1	58.8	46.3	43.9	43.9	50.7	24.3	24.6	22.1	24.9	63.1	63.4	66.0	72.5	28.9	30.2	39.5	41.5
Weak opponents	27.4	27.0	25.4	18.0	16.0	14.6	16.9	14.8	21.1	19.8	19.9	15.3	3.8	10.4	9.7	7.7	24.3	32.0	25.4	24.9
Strong opponents	15.0	13.8	17.1	13.2	16.1	17.5	20.4	12.2	15.6	13.4	14.4	12.1	2.6	5.3	5.7	4.3	25.8	24.0	18.7	16.4
No. of cases	1069	1009	1003	1040	1088	1015	1001	971	1197	992	987	1202	1174	1060	1102	1011	1256	1042	1055	957
Missing cases	31	35	42	27	20	16	15	19	169	122	106	117	63	57	60	32	76	39	51	58

Sources: Commission of the European Communities, Eurobarometer nos. 17, 21, 25, 31a. Tables taken from Fuchs and Rucht (1994).

There is additional information that helps even better to understand the potential impact of the new social movement cadres. About one quarter of those respondents who support the ecology, anti–nuclear power, or peace movements, support the other two equally. The situation is such that one observes a core of potential activists that is ready to move on any issue pertinent to one of the three movements, thereby thoroughly enhancing the aggregate mobilization potential and expertise of the new social movements. Furthermore, movement elites no longer act separately from other, established corporate actors, such as political parties and trade unions. A study has documented for the Netherlands the degree to which the new social movements are already linked to those established actors, and thereby also have opened up a direct channel of influence on governmental decision-making.[10]

In summary, while anxieties about mass politics as nonmediated politics are not sustained by the available empirical evidence, the observed differentiation and augmentation of intermediary structures may well be in line with a process of individualization through which people on an ad hoc basis participate for some (probably limited) period of time in those intermediary organizations that best suit their present goal priorities. This element of choice potentially creates an instability in the intermediation process, which makes political outcomes less predictable and less tied to established corporate actors still at the core of the institutionalized political process. Consequently, it becomes ever more important to understand the new cleavages and issues resulting from the far-reaching sociopolitical changes addressed before. The next section will deal with the extent to which these changes may have had an impact on the values people hold, an important element in this respect, for values are the second factor in the heuristic causal chain.

4. VALUE CHANGE IN WESTERN EUROPE

With his seminal article on the silent revolution in Europe, Ronald Inglehart has triggered a heated scholarly debate on the shift of individual value preferences as a result of continuing economic well-being and growth in industrial societies after the Second World War.[11] The controversies about Inglehart's concept are legion and need not be reexamined here.[12] Undoubtedly, his speculation that as societies advance in wealth and personal security, materialist values decline and new, postmaterialist values such as self-actualization and participation consistently gain in importance has found considerable supporting evidence and has even been incorporated into the public discourse of many Western societies.

When Inglehart first formulated his hypothesis in 1971, a major weakness of his approach was that the longitudinal data necessary to decide whether the postulated change was a generational or a life-cycle phenomenon were not yet available. One of Inglehart's notable achievements is that through his early established ties with the Eurobarometer group, he was able to incorporate the four items on which his basic measurement instrument relies into all Eurobarometers. This has since permitted him to perform the kind of longitudinal analysis necessary, especially for assessing whether observed age differences in value preferences were due to life-cycle or generational effects.

To answer this question reliably is important because of its societal implications. The preponderance of a life-cycle effect—that is, age differences being a consequence of individuals' positions in their life cycle— would lead to an approximate aggregate stability of the orientations in question. A generational effect, on the other hand, would imply that as societies move on through time, they change in aggregate orientations.

These analyses have resulted in reliable findings (see figure 4) that, as Inglehart had predicted, age differences in value orientations in postindustrial societies do generally exist, and most of these differences are of a generational nature, with some additional period effects (that is, historical events that influence all birth cohorts more or less equally).[13]

Figure 4 is informative on two counts. First, it shows in detail the generational effects in plotting the value preferences of eight birth cohorts across time, emphasizing both the difference of degree of postmaterialism across the cohorts (the younger cohorts being more postmaterialist) and the maintenance of the observed differences between cohorts across time— the generational effect. Second, figure 4 indicates that period effects of sizable magnitude also exist. The superimposition of the inflation rate in the figure was chosen by Inglehart and Abramson to demonstrate that the formulation of one of the value items ("fight rising prices") makes the postmaterialism index especially vulnerable to period effects related to inflation.

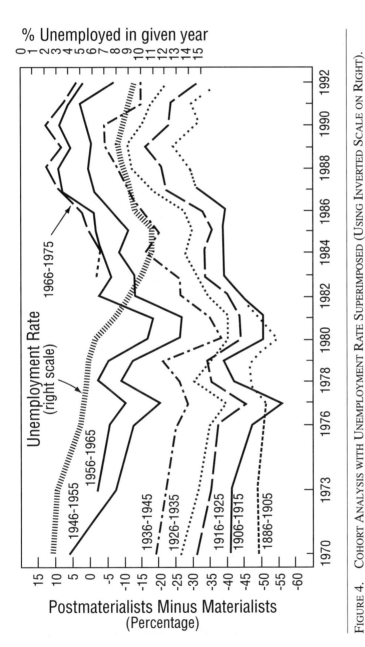

FIGURE 4. COHORT ANALYSIS WITH UNEMPLOYMENT RATE SUPERIMPOSED (USING INVERTED SCALE ON RIGHT).

Sources: Combined weighted representative national surveys from France, West Germany, Britain, Italy, Belgium, and the Netherlands, including European Community surveys from 1970 and 1973 and *Eurobarometer* surveys 6 through 37 (over 220,000 interviews). Figure taken from Ronald Inglehart and Paul R. Abramson, "Economic Security and Value Change," *American Political Science Review* 88 (1994), pp. 336–54.

Note: Percentage postmaterialist — percentage materialist in six West European societies.

For speculations about the future of postmaterialism, it is interesting to notice in figure 4 that the economic strains that have surfaced in Western Europe since 1990 apparently have also left their mark on these values. If one were to argue in line with Inglehart, one might say that what can be empirically established is a classical period effect that will disappear as the economies of the West pick up steam again. However, equally plausible may be the idea that the strains that have surfaced in the West for some years now, and that reach far beyond the limited field of the economy, are more than just a passing fancy. Thus, the dip in the postmaterialism index may turn out to be more than just a period effect. This, though, only the future can tell.

At the core of the Inglehart approach lies the concept of the law of diminishing marginal utility, combined with a socialization hypothesis. For 35 countries for which data on postmaterialism are available, figure 5 plots the average economic growth rate from 1950 to 1990 against the (gamma) correlation between age and postmaterialism.[14] These data indicate that there is remarkable cross-national substance to Inglehart's claim that the road to postmaterialism is intricately intertwined with economic growth. For Western Europe, this fact is once more corroborated by figures 6 and 7, which divide the 12 EU members into seven economically well-developed and five less developed countries. This difference is reflected well in the absolute levels of postmaterialism in the two sets. The overall growth in postmaterialism visible in these figures, however, speaks once more to the generational replacement model figuring so prominently in the Inglehart analysis.

German research indicates that it was in the late 1960s that values experienced their first, quite sudden and substantial change.[15] The lack of reliable cross-national data makes it difficult to assess whether German findings hold true for other countries, and what the driving forces behind that change were. There exists at least some evidence to support the notion that an Inglehart-type value change in Europe is related to a process of secularization in the double sense of a truly dramatic turning of the people away from the churches and also from traditional religious beliefs. This process apparently started in Protestant countries in the 1950s; with some time lag, it has by now been embraced by the predominantly Catholic countries as well (figures 8 and 9). Given the substantial reach of religious convictions as a unifying element in people's belief systems, there is every reason to assume that

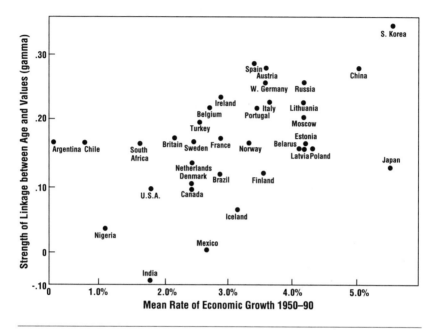

FIGURE 5. DIFFERENCES BETWEEN THE VALUES OF YOUNG AND OLD IN SOCIETIES WITH DIFFERING RATES OF ECONOMIC GROWTH

Sources: 1990–1991 World Value Survey. Figure taken from Inglehart and Abramson, "Economic Security and Value Change."
Notes: $r = .52$; $p < .001$; based on the 12-item index of materialist/postmaterialist values. Data on economic growth were not available for Bulgaria, Czechoslovakia, East Germany, Hungary, or Northern Ireland.

this process of secularization—which cannot be registered equally in the United States—has had a far-reaching and general impact on the belief systems of West European citizens.[16]

Of course, especially in the context of this study, the question should be raised: What are the consequences of the change in value orientations for political orientations in general and attitudes toward transatlantic relations in particular? Initially, two related answers can be given.

The first is that in the early 1970s not only public value preferences but also the political agenda in the West European states began to change. The emerging issues of the environment and of greater participation of the people in decision-making are two cases in point. Tables 9 and 10 shed

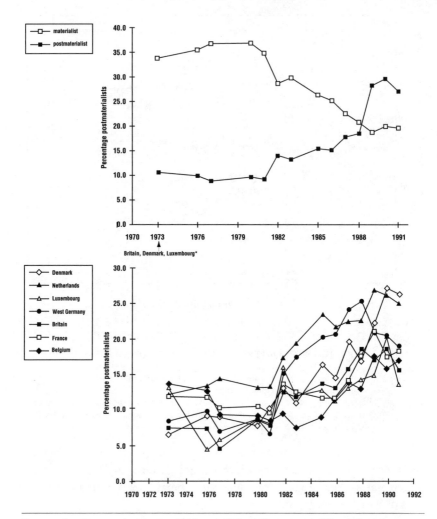

FIGURE 6.   POSTMATERIALISM IN SEVEN MORE ADVANCED WEST EUROPEAN
COUNTRIES 1973–91 (ANNUALIZED PERCENTAGES)

Sources: Commission of the European Communities, *Eurobarometer* (1993b), cumulated
data (1973–91). Figure taken from Scarbrough (1995).
*In 1973 Britain, Denmark, and Luxembourg entered the common market.

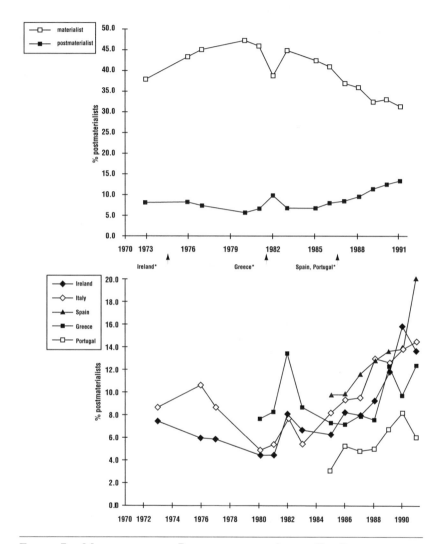

FIGURE 7. MATERIALISM AND POSTMATERIALISM AMONG FIVE LESS
ADVANCED INDUSTRIAL SOCIETIES IN THE EUROPEAN COMMUNITY
1970–91 (MEAN PERCENTAGES)

Sources: Commission of the European Communities, *Eurobarometer*, cumulated data
(1973–91). Figure taken from Scarbrough (1993).

*Indicates when country entered the common market.

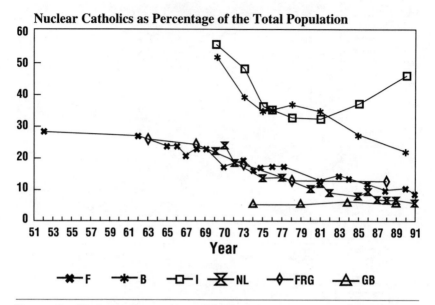

FIGURE 8.   NUCLEAR CATHOLICS IN SIX WEST EUROPEAN COUNTRIES 1951–91

Sources: Belgium and Italy: EC studies and *Eurobarometer* studies. France: data made
   available by Yves Lambert, Centre National de Recherche Scientifique, Groupe
   de Sociologie de Religion, Paris. Britain: British election studies and British
   social attitudes surveys. Netherlands: national election studies and cultural
   change survey. West Germany: social surveys and various other studies.
   Figure taken from Jagodzinski and Dobbleaere (1995).

some light on the consequences of changes in value orientations (on citizens' issue priorities, the data only covers the period from 1976 onwards
because earlier cross-national data are not available).

   The most striking and cross-nationally valid finding in table 9 is that
by the mid-1970s the issues of the "new" political agenda had already thoroughly permeated the "old" agenda. In those few countries where in 1976
the old agenda retained at least some weight, such weight had been further
reduced by 1987 almost to the point of nonexistence. In passing, it should
be mentioned that this result lends force to critical arguments put forward
by Helmut Klages that Inglehart's conceptualization of value change is de-
ficient in one core respect: by fiat (through the rank-order method used by
Inglehart in obtaining measurements for his postmaterialism index) the

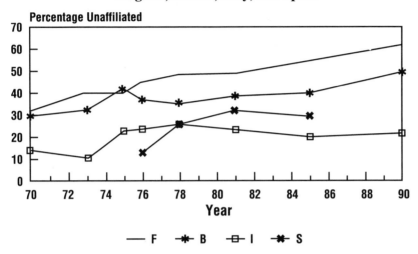

A. Catholic Countries, 1970–90
Belgium, France, Italy, and Spain

Percentage Unaffiliated

— F   —✳— B   —☐— I   —✴— S

B. Protestant/Mixed Countries, 1959–90
Denmark, Great Britain, Netherlands, and West Germany

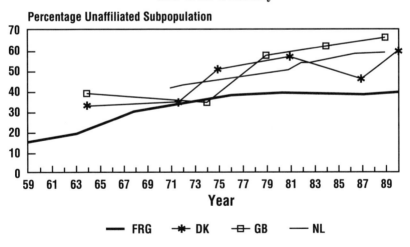

Percentage Unaffiliated Subpopulation

— FRG   —✳— DK   —☐— GB   — NL

FIGURE 9.   CHURCH DISENGAGEMENT IN EIGHT WEST EUROPEAN COUNTRIES

Sources: Denmark: Danish data archives. Spain: Officinade Estadistica y Sociologia de la Iglesia. West Germany: election studies. For other countries, see figure 8. Figure taken from Jagodzinski and Dobbelaere (1995).

TABLE 9. DEVELOPMENT OF INDIVIDUAL AGENDAS 1976–87

Political Agendas	Denmark				Belgium				Great Britain				West Germany			
	1976	1978	1983	1987	1976	1978	1983	1987	1976	1978	1983	1987	1974	1976	1983	1987
Old (security, economic) + new agendas	59	57	56	53	47	47	56	45	56	59	73	61	54	49	56	52
Old agenda (security, economic)	2	2	5	3	1	4	2	2	14	16	8	8	6	10	6	2
Old (security) + new agendas	1	—	1	1	—	1	1	1	1	1	1	1	—	4	1	1
Old (economic) + new agendas	37	39	34	39	47	43	35	40	22	17	16	24	31	26	33	41
Single agenda or no agenda	1	2	4	4	5	5	6	12	7	7	2	6	9	11	4	4

Political Agendas	Ireland				Luxembourg				Netherlands				France			
	1976	1978	1983	1987	1976	1978	1983	1987	1976	1978	1983	1987	1976	1978	1983	1987
Old (security, economic) + new agendas	68	61	55	45	36	28	29	46	63	52	49	38	64	59	68	66
Old agenda (security, economic)	2	5	2	4	3	4	—	—	3	2	4	3	1	1	3	4
Old (security) + new agendas	—	—	1	—	1	1	—	—	1	—	—	—	1	—	1	—
Old (economic) + new agendas	26	28	36	40	56	51	65	48	30	44	41	51	33	38	25	26
Single agenda or no agenda	4	6	6	11	4	16	6	6	3	2	6	8	1	2	3	4

	Italy			Greece			Spain	Portugal	Average			
	1976	1978	1983	1987	1983	1987	1987	1987	1976	1978	1983	1987
Old (security, economic) + new agendas	57	49	52	54	88	86	71	. 69	56	51	55	51
Old agenda (security, economic)	1	1	2	1	1	1	—	1	4	5	4	3
Old (security) + new agendas	—	—	1	1	1	1	—	—	1	1	1	—
Old (economic) + new agendas	40	47	41	40	9	11	24	27	36	37	36	39
Single agenda or no agenda	2	3	4	4	1	1	5	2	4	6	5	7

Sources: Commission of the European Communities, *Eurobarometer* nos. 6 (1976), 10 (1978), 20 (1983), 28 (1987). Table taken from Roller (1995).

Notes: Entries are percentage of respondents who consider this agenda as very important or important. The average figure excludes Greece, Spain, and Portugal. Old agenda (security) = mean of "military defense" and "defend interests against superpowers," old agenda (economic) = "fighting unemployment," new agenda = mean of "reducing the number of very rich and very poor people," "reducing differences between regions," and "fighting pollution."

TABLE 10. OLD POLITICS AGENDA (SECURITY) AND POLITICAL ORIENTATION: CHANGE 1976–87

	Denmark			Belgium			Britain		
	1976	1987	Change	1976	1987	Change	1976	1987	Change
Materialist left	58	50	−8	45	46	1	73	68	−5
Postmaterialist left	42	37	−5	43	45	2	62	58	−4
Materialist right	75	70	−5	49	47	−2	72	81	9
Postmaterialist right	68	70	2	55	48	−7	77	75	−2

	Germany			Ireland			Luxembourg		
	1976	1987	Change	1976	1987	Change	1976	1987	Change
Materialist left	63	54	−9	70	48	−22	29	48	19
Postmaterialist left	39	36	−3	63	49	−14	45	36	−9
Materialist right	66	73	7	74	53	−21	29	49	20
Postmaterialist right	61	56	−5	67	48	−19	62	47	−15

	Netherlands			France			Italy		
	1976	1987	Change	1976	1987	Change	1976	1987	Change
Materialist left	68	34	−34	61	74	13	49	54	5
Postmaterialist left	48	25	−23	56	52	−4	53	46	−7
Materialist right	75	56	−19	80	79	−1	66	66	0
Postmaterialist right	76	43	−33	73	81	8	61	62	1

	Greece 1987	Spain 1987	Portugal 1987	Average 1976	Average 1987	Change
Materialist Left	89	77	73	57	53	−4
Postmaterialist Left	88	80	65	50	43	−7
Materialist Right	91	69	100	65	64	−1
Postmaterialist Right	82	59	100	67	59	−8

Sources: Commission of the European Communities, *Eurobarometer* nos. 6 (1976) and 28 (1987). Table taken from Roller (1995).
Notes: Entries are percentage of respondents who consider this agenda as very important or important. Security is the mean of "military defenses" and "defend interest against superpowers." The average figure excludes Greece, Spain, and Portugal.

most interesting part of the value change process is missed—the synthesis of materialist and postmaterialist values within individuals.[17]

Furthermore, it appears from the "old" political agenda that the security issue is disproportionately losing impact on people's issue priorities. This finding would probably be even more pronounced if data for a more recent year than 1987 were available. In addition, table 10 is well in line with previous analyses that of the four value/ideology types in the table, it is the postmaterialist left that ranks by far the lowest in security agenda priority. Here it has to be borne in mind, though, that on average, for all of the value/ideology types, a decrease in security agenda priority can be observed.

The second answer to the question regarding the political consequences of the observed change in value orientations for transatlantic relations deals with the rise of the Green parties and the transformation of traditional social-democratic parties. As postmaterialists on the average are young, ideologically to the left, and well educated, they have from the beginning been trying very hard to get "their" issues on the political agenda. They have been successful in this in two ways. The empirical evidence is overwhelming that the younger segment of the postmaterialists became active in the new social movements in the 1970s, particularly on behalf of the environment. Here lies the nucleus for the emergence of the Green parties (the pervasive impact of this development on the rise of Green parties in Western Europe is well documented in Mueller-Rommel).[18] The other, somewhat older postmaterialists of the 1968 student revolutionary-type made their way—to paraphrase German student leader Rudi Dutschke—by marching through the established political institutions, especially the social-democratic parties. The internal bifurcation of many West European social-democratic parties into an "old left" wing and a "new left" wing testifies to the impact of postmaterialist thinking.

At the beginning of this section it was argued that one element of the change in value orientation has been the desire of large parts of the West European electorates to have a greater say in political and social matters. Improved education and the erosion of belief in authority through secularization are probably the most important corollaries of the "participatory revolution" that have taken place in Western democracies. This topic will be addressed next.

5. THE PARTICIPATORY REVOLUTION

One of the concerns growing from the politically difficult times between the two world wars in Europe was ambivalence concerning political participation. On the one hand, high rates of political involvement could be interpreted as indicators for a correspondingly high identification with the polity. On the other hand, evidence from the Weimar Republic, for instance, showed that high and increasing political participation was a sign of severe strain, which could have helped to pave the way for totalitarianism.

Correspondingly, for two decades after the Second World War the interpretation prevailed in political science that a certain amount of political apathy was not at all detrimental and perhaps even beneficial to the democratic process. In a somewhat sophisticated fashion, civic culture was regarded as the optimal combination of elements of citizen quiescence and activity.

The student movements of the 1960s around the democratic world, which started out by demanding more say in university decision-making, radically challenged this point of view for the first time since the war. It did not take long to generalize the idea that democratic politics required more direct citizen participation than was constitutionally anticipated through the vote in most democracies. The resulting rise in popularity of direct political action began in the early 1970s and since then has spread, as political action studies and related analyses have shown.[19]

There are three distinct developments that need to be taken up in this context. First, it was not entirely clear at the beginning whether demands for more political influence were aimed at transforming the existing liberal democracies in a socialist direction or at enhancing input into the political process. Second, it was initially an open question to what extent modern democracies were facing but an ephemeral protest phenomenon or a general change toward more participation above and beyond the existing provisions for voting participation. Third, it remained to be seen whether these changes would persist and even increase as time went by.

The first two questions can be easily answered. As empirical evidence for these new political phenomena began to accumulate, it quickly became apparent that the demand for more participatory channels seldom implied visions of a radically transformed political system. Rather, more participation came to be understood by most people as enhancing the potential legitimacy of present democracy. Regarding the protest element, there can be no doubt that noninstitutionalized forms of political participation are used most frequently to express dissatisfaction with specific government policies, particularly at the local level. In many ways, this reflects the decrease in ideology resulting from weakening ties between individual citizens and their parties. However, beyond this, the increased use and therefore normality of noninstitutionalized political participation has, in a structural fashion, opened up and stabilized new avenues for citizens to make themselves heard politically. This implication goes far beyond a simplistic protest notion of political participation.

Regarding the third question, it is easy to muster impressive empirical evidence that in the last 30 years almost all West European democracies have experienced a substantial rise in citizens' political involvement (table 11). This involvement basically can take two forms: an increased political repertory, in the sense of commanding a wide variety of political actions, which can be tailored to any given issue; and increased political participation. While there are important differences between the two, especially regarding the process of mobilization into real action, research has shown that—with the exception of age, which is more strongly correlated with intent than action—contemporary political participation outside established channels is driven by a similar and cross-nationally comparable set of factors: high education, high political interest, postmaterialism, and leftism (see table 12 for actual participation in legal uninstitutionalized modes of action and table 13 for basic willingness to participate). By now, the new social movements have become the most telling organizational expression of this development.

Adopting a long-range perspective, described changes in participatory orientations have not yet—contrary to some allegations—drastically diminished the inclination of the electorate to participate in elections, the democratic mode of expressing overarching political preferences. Nevertheless, findings on noninstitutionalized political participation regarding the ideological, value, and resource background of the actors involved may well give rise to concerns about political equality, precisely because of the issue selectivity of these active partial publics. Beyond this question of normative democratic theory, contemporary political elites simply have to take into account these participatory orientations when making political decisions. In fact, there is ample evidence that this is exactly what they have been doing for some time.

TABLE 11.   POLITICAL PARTICIPATION IN WESTERN EUROPE 1959–90

	1959	1974	1981	1990
None	85	69	55	44
Some	11	27	38	46
Active	4	4	7	10
N	(2,734)	(6,148)	(13,315)	(15,107)

Note: Entries are aggregate percentages. All the original data have been reanalyzed.

POLITICAL PARTICIPATION IN WESTERN EUROPE (BY COUNTRY) 1959–90

	1959	1974	1981	1990
Denmark	—	—	48	59
Finland	—	26	40	38
Iceland	—	—	40	55
Norway	—	—	58	68
Sweden	—	—	58	74
Belgium	—	—	27	51
Britain	18	31	66	77
Ireland	—	—	32	46
Netherlands	—	28	37	54
West Germany	16	34	48	57
France	—	—	52	57
Italy	10	34	50	56
Spain	—	—	32	32

Sources: Civic Culture (1959); Political Action (1973–76); European Values Survey (1981); World Value Survey (1990). Tables taken from Topf (1995).

Note: Entries are percentage of adult population who engage in some form of political participation beyond voting.

TABLE 12. REGRESSIONS OF TWO SETS OF INDEPENDENT VARIABLES ON LEGAL NONINSTITUTIONALIZED PARTICIPATION I IN THE 12 EC COUNTRIES IN 1989: B'S AND BETAS

Independent variables	Countries											
	F	GB	D	I	NL	DK	B	L	IRL	GR	E	P
SET 1: SOCIODEMOGRAPHIC VARIABLES												
Education	.09	.06	.10	.07	.05	.03	.04	-.08	.04	.07	.08	.10
	(.22)	(.17)	(.25)	(.19)	(.14)	(.07)	(.09)	(.19)	(.11)	(.19)	(.21)	(.23)
Gender	-.07	.03	-.06	-.21	.03	-.03	-.06	.22	-.12	-.37	-.22	.04
	(-.03)	(.02)	(-.03)	(-.10)	(.02)	(-.01)	(-.02)	(.10)	(-.07)	(-.17)	(-.09)	(.02)
Age	.00	-.00	-.00	.00	-.00	-.00	-.00	-.00	-.00	.00	.00	.00
	(.09)	(-.00)	(-.07)	(.00)	(-.11)	(-.06)	(-.02)	(-.04)	(-.06)	(.07)	(.03)	(.10)
SET 2: ATTITUDINAL VARIABLES												
Left-right self-placement	-.08	-.08	-.10	-.11	-.11	-.15	-.08	-.03	-.09	-.08	-.08	-.10
	(-.15)	(-.20)	(-.19)	(-.21)	(-.25)	(-.30)	(-.14)	(-.07)	(-.19)	(-.19)	(-.16)	(-.19)
Political interest	-.31	-.26	-.25	-.32	-.17	-.27	-.31	-.32	-.18	-.28	-.21	-.32
	(-.24)	(-.24)	(-.19)	(-.25)	(-.15)	(-.19)	(-.26)	(-.24)	(-.19)	(-.23)	(-.18)	(-.25)
MAT-POSTMAT	-.16	-.11	-.17	-.17	-.18	-.15	-.10	-.05	-.02	-.05	-.15	-.03
	(-.16)	(-.12)	(-.18)	(-.16)	(-.19)	(-.14)	(-.09)	(-.05)	(-.03)	(-.04)	(-.14)	(-.03)
Multiple R^2 set 1	.11	.06	.08	.13	.09	.06	.06	.09	.06	.13	.13	.08
Multiple R^2 set 2	.19	.14	.17	.25	.17	.21	.14	.11	.10	.15	.18	.12
Multiple R^2 sets 1–2	.25	.17	.20	.29	.21	.22	.15	.15	.12	.21	.22	.17

Source: Max Kaase, "Direct Political Participation in the Late Eighties in the EU Countries," in P. Gundelach and R. Sivne, eds., *From Voters to Participants* (Aarkus: Politice, 1992), p. 87.
Note: Betas are in parentheses.

TABLE 13.   REGRESSIONS OF TWO SETS OF INDEPENDENT VARIABLES ON LEGAL NONINSTITUTIONALIZED PARTICIPATION III IN THE 12 EC COUNTRIES IN 1989: B'S AND BETAS

| | Countries | | | | | | | | | | | |
Independent variables	F	GB	D	I	NL	DK	B	L	IRL	GR	E	P
SET 1: SOCIODEMOGRAPHIC VARIABLES												
Education	.08	.07	.06	.05	.11	.06	.12	.16	.04	.06	.06	.10
	(.18)	(.15)	(.11)	(.14)	(.23)	(.11)	(.22)	(.28)	(.07)	(.15)	(.15)	(.16)
Gender	−.13	−.16	−.17	−.11	−.17	−.22	−.14	.06	−.27	−.41	−.27	−.37
	(−.05)	(−.07)	(−.06)	(−.05)	(−.06)	(−.08)	(−.05)	(.02)	(−.11)	(−.17)	(−.10)	(−.12)
Age	−.00	.00	−.01	−.01	−.02	−.03	−.01	−.01	−.02	−.01	−.02	.00
	(−.13)	(.13)	(−.17)	(−.19)	(−.28)	(−.32)	(−.13)	(−.13)	(−.22)	(−.15)	(−.25)	(.00)
SET 2: ATTITUDINAL VARIABLES												
Left-right self-placement	−.07	−.10	−.07	−.07	−.07	−.15	−.09	−.09	−.05	−.06	−.05	−.14
	(−.13)	(−.17)	(−.09)	(−.13)	(−.11)	(−.23)	(−.12)	(−.14)	(−.08)	(−.12)	(−.09)	(−.17)
Political interest	−.36	−.29	−.26	−.32	−.21	−.30	−.18	−.11	−.27	−.18	−.29	−.12
	(−.27)	(−.20)	(−.15)	(−.24)	(−.12)	(−.16)	(−.12)	(−.06)	(−.21)	(−.13)	(−.22)	(−.06)
MAT-POSTMAT	−.16	−.10	−.20	−.16	−.22	−.18	−.13	−.09	−.01	−.14	−.11	−.21
	(−.15)	(−.08)	(−.15)	(−.14)	(−.16)	(−.12)	(−.10)	(−.06)	(−.01)	(−.12)	(−.09)	(−.13)
Multiple R² set 1	.13	.09	.10	.17	.23	.22	.16	.18	.11	.16	.29	.07
Multiple R² set 2	.20	.11	.11	.20	.15	.21	.11	.10	.06	.11	.20	.08
Multiple R² sets 1 + 2	.26	.17	.16	.27	.30	.34	.19	.19	.14	.19	.28	.12

Source: Max Kaase, "Direct Political Participation in the Late Eighties in the EU Countries," p. 88.
Note: Betas are in parentheses.

6. THE LEGITIMACY QUESTION

In the 1970s German and European political science was confronted, on purely nonempirical grounds, with speculations about the imminent breakdown of the late-bourgeois democratic state. This idea finally arrived in the United States at a time when political science had already diagnosed a decline in political trust that had started in the 1960s.[20] Later research concluded that this decline did not impinge on the identification of American citizens with their principles of democratic government.[21] This was the time when, in Europe, empirical research came up with initial findings diametrically opposed to the speculation that Western democracies were undergoing a severe crisis of legitimacy.

To conduct good empirical research on political legitimacy is a scholarly challenge because of the conceptual complexity innate to the subject. To this day, cross-national longitudinal data on political legitimacy, which would permit reliable scholarly answers to the questions involved in this broad topic, are still unavailable. German findings, at least, indicate that citizens are indeed capable of validly distinguishing between various objects (political authorities, political regime, political community) and modes (specific support, diffuse support) of legitimacy beliefs.[22] These analytical distinctions, derived from the work of David Easton, are very important because they pertain to the core logic of political elite competition in pluralist democracies ("throwing the rascals out") and to the idea that it is this competition and the institutionalized option of governmental change that serve as a buffer against the possibility of dissatisfaction with the reigning political authorities being generalized to the level of the (democratic) political regime and its central institutions, norms, and values.[23]

This conceptual concern is relevant for the evaluation of the few extant cross-national data on political legitimacy beliefs. Unfortunately, the only pertinent survey question available can be found in the Eurobarometers, and this question (see figure 10) is flawed in the sense that it mixes elements of the regime dimension (democracy) with elements of the authorities dimension (works in your country). Since these elements cannot be disentangled in a satisfactory manner, one simply has to live with the available indicator, bearing in mind the conceptual ambivalence just mentioned.

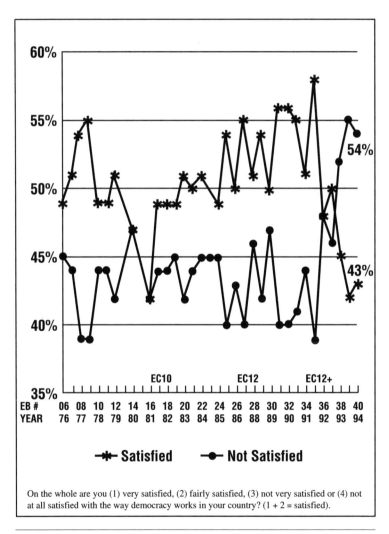

FIGURE 10.   SATISFIED WITH DEMOCRACY IN ONE'S COUNTRY?
1976–93 (EUROPEAN COMMUNITY-12)

Source: European Commission, *Eurobarometer.*

Regarding the question, posed in the introductory part of this section, of whether a crisis of legitimacy exists or existed in Western Europe, the data in table 14 give a differentiated answer: for the period 1976–91 such a pervasive crisis cannot in general be found.[24] However, there are substantial differences between countries in trends and, much more pronounced, in levels of legitimacy. When one considers the criterion of statistical significance, then in Denmark, Belgium, the United Kingdom, Ireland, and Spain, no change in legitimacy can be detected. Only Germany and Greece suffer a loss, whereas in the remaining six countries substantial gains are recorded.

One has to bear in mind, though, that the above analysis ends with the year 1991. As the results from 1992 onwards show, the EU countries as a whole have, in the second half of 1992, experienced a truly precipitous decline in the level of satisfaction with the workings of their national

TABLE 14. TRENDS OF SATISFACTION WITH DEMOCRACY IN
13 WEST EUROPEAN COUNTRIES 1976–91
(LINEAR REGRESSION ON TIME)

Countries:	B	Standard Error	Beta	R Square
Denmark	(.03)	.12	(.28)	.08
Belgium	(.04)	.15	.26	.07
Britain	(−.02)	.29	(−.20)	.04
Germany	(−.03)	.11	(−.29)	.09
Ireland	(−.02)	.45	−.14	.02
Northern Ireland	(.10)	.00	.65	.43
Luxembourg	(.06)	.00	.52	.27
Netherlands	(.06)	.03	.39	.15
France	(.04)	.07	.33	.11
Italy	(.08)	.00	.76	.58
Greece	(−.14)	.00	−.63	.39
Spain	(.06)	.44	.24	.06
Portugal	(.30)	.04	.58	.33

Sources: Commission of the European Communities, *Eurobarometer* nos. 6–35. Table taken from Fuchs, Guidorossi, and Svensson (1995).

democracies, a decline far below the lowest level ever measured since 1973. In 1993 those dissatisfied outnumbered those satisfied, as in early 1994.

It is not yet possible to muster a reliable interpretation regarding the meaning of this decline. Most likely, what can be observed since 1992 is an interaction effect between the loss of communism as a countervailing yet stablizing ideology for democracy, and dissatisfaction with the economic crisis in Western Europe. However, even if one is willing to accept this argument, most of this decline in satisfaction is directed at the governments presently in power in the various EU member states, not against the democratic system as such. Yet these data certainly give cause for concern.

7. ATTITUDES TOWARD THE EUROPEAN UNION

Almost all of the literature on the conditions under which nation-states integrate into new, transnational units emphasizes—over and above many other factors—the role of elites in this process. In the case of the European Union, this can be most clearly seen by the relatively low support for the EU in Denmark and Great Britain, before as well as after their entry into the EU, when this was still a controversial issue between the major political parties in these countries.

Under conditions of low public saliency and high elite support (which usually translate into friendly mass media coverage), it can be expected that the majority of the publics will be supportive of, or at least indifferent to, issues related to transnational state building. This is exactly what happened for an extended period in the case of the European Union, as the respective Eurobarometer data show.

For obvious reasons the Eurobarometers have from the beginning tapped attitudes toward the EU in the respective member countries. In the Eurobarometer reports published biannually by the Commission, responses to four indicators are always displayed and discussed, which all pertain to attitudes toward European unification as crystallized in the EU.[25] The four questions are:

1. Attitude toward European Unification

   In general, are you for or against efforts being made to unify Western Europe? Are you (1) very much for, (2) to some extent for, (3) to some extent against, (4) or very much against efforts being made to unify Western Europe?

(1 + 2 = unification)

2. Attitude toward Membership in the European Union

Generally speaking, do you think that [our country's] membership in the European Union is (1) a good thing, (2) a bad thing, or (3) neither good nor bad?

(1 = membership)

3. Evaluation of Benefit from European Union Membership

Taking everything into consideration, would you say that [our country] has on balance (1) benefited or (2) not benefited from being a member of the European Union?

(1 = benefit)

4. Attitude toward Dissolution of the European Union

If you were told tomorrow that the European Union had been scrapped, would you be (1) very sorry about it, (2) indifferent, or (3) relieved?

(1 = regret dissolution)

Figures 11–17 display developments with respect to these four indicators between 1981 and 1993 for the EU-12 as a whole and individual member countries. (There is no point in discussing the development of these attitudes in the individual countries here.) Detailed analyses of these data by Niedermayer[26] first of all point out that, given the substantial share of undecided or indifferent responses, reporting only the EU-favorable responses (as in figures 11–17) may create a misleading impression of the evolution of EU attitudes, if negative or indifferent answers are not taken into consideration.[27] Second, Niedermayer shows that attitudes toward the EU follow distinctively different time patterns.[28] Between 1978 and 1980, a small anti-EU tendency, which probably reflected the stagnation in the integration process, could be observed. This was followed by a uniform trend toward Europeanization between 1981 and 1985, before the publics of the six "old" EU member states and the six "new" member states parted ways. Whereas support for European integration and for the EU in the ini-

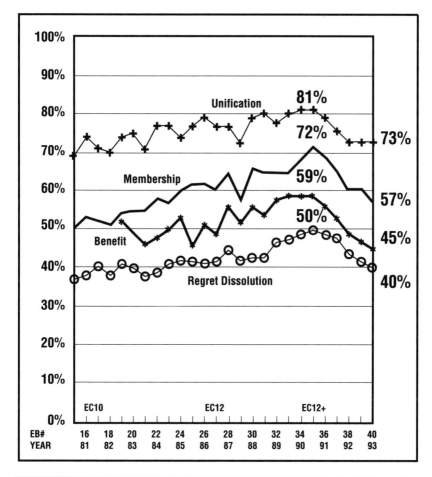

FIGURE 11.   SUPPORT FOR EUROPEAN INTEGRATION AND THE COMMUNITY
(EUROPEAN COMMUNITY-12) 1981–93

Source: European Commission, *Eurobarometer.*

tial group of six countries stagnated or declined, in the newer member states
(including Denmark and Great Britain) a clear increase in support took
place. Consequently, the overall slight increase in pro-EU attitudes in the
EU as a whole (see figure 11) has to be taken with a grain of salt.

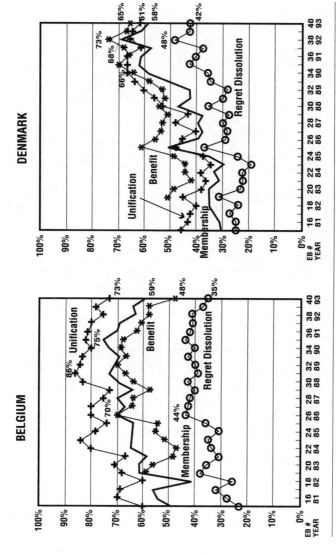

FIGURE 12.   SUPPORT FOR EUROPEAN INTEGRATION AND THE COMMUNITY 1981–93

Source: European Commission, *Eurobarometer.*

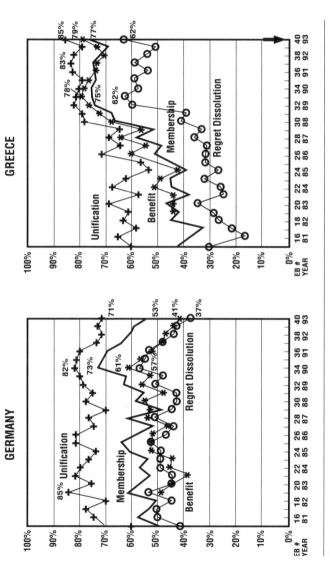

FIGURE 13.   SUPPORT FOR EUROPEAN INTEGRATION AND THE COMMUNITY 1981–93

Source: European Commission, *Eurobarometer.*

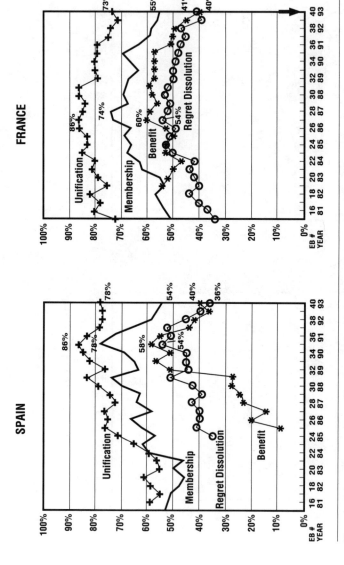

FIGURE 14. SUPPORT FOR EUROPEAN INTEGRATION AND THE COMMUNITY 1981–93

Source: European Commission, *Eurobarometer.*

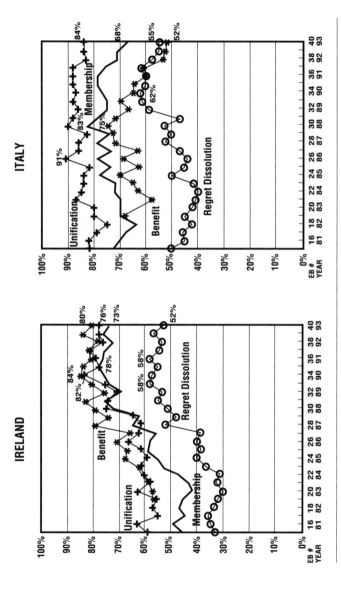

FIGURE 15. SUPPORT FOR EUROPEAN INTEGRATION AND THE COMMUNITY 1981–93

Source: European Commission, *Eurobarometer.*

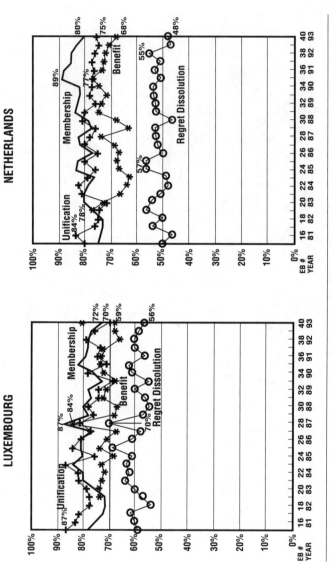

FIGURE 16. SUPPORT FOR EUROPEAN INTEGRATION AND THE COMMUNITY 1981–93

Source: European Commission, *Eurobarometer.*

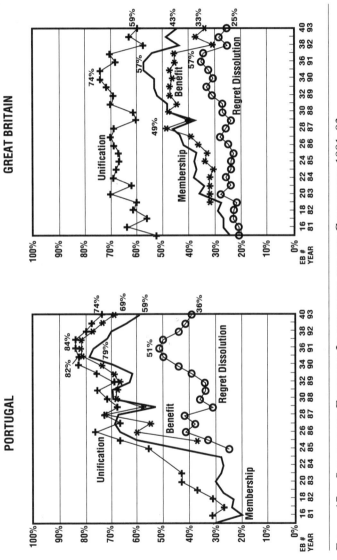

FIGURE 17. SUPPORT FOR EUROPEAN INTEGRATION AND THE COMMUNITY 1981–93.

Source: European Commission, *Eurobarometer.*

The most interesting aspect of the development of EU-related attitudes concerns the 1991–93 period, which was characterized by a pervasive, uniform, and rather substantial decrease in EU support, with the exception of Ireland; this process continued in early 1994. It is difficult to assess precisely the causes of this weakening of the pro-EU mood. Most likely, one of the major causes was the Maastricht Treaty of February 7, 1992, which set the stage for concrete steps toward creating a political union by the end of the century. Data from the Eurobarometer of June 1993 show that the public of EU member states did not know a great deal about this treaty at that time (figure 18). Nevertheless, many did not hesitate to venture a pro- or contra-Maastricht opinion, if a referendum on that question took place. If one correlates the answers to these two questions, then a very intriguing picture emerges. Of the 16 percent of the EU-12 public believing to be well informed about Maastricht, this treaty was supported by 61 percent, and not supported by 23 percent, with 16 percent undecided. The lower the level of information, the less *support for and rejection of* the treaty declined and the higher the number of people undecided on the matter became. If one is willing to extrapolate from these findings, one conclusion would be—other things being equal—that as information on the Maastricht Treaty grew, so acceptance and rejection both increased, leading to a further polarization in EU matters that might well have some impact on the general acceptance of the EU and further European unification. In this sense, Maastricht may indeed constitute a watershed for the further development of the Union.

Such structuring of data seems to reflect a situation of informational insecurity on the part of the majority of people, on the one hand, and by a growing awareness of the implications of a unification process pushed forward by political elites, on the other. This process is apparently epitomized by the issue of a common European currency and—slightly less so—by that of a European Central Bank. It almost appears that as the consequences of the process toward European integration are finally beginning to be felt by citizens with respect to everyday issues, many people previously vaguely supportive of or indifferent to European unification and the EU are now beginning to become more skeptical about them—the symbolic politics of "giving up one's currency" may also enter the picture. This is the more likely scenario, as there is precious little evidence available that something resembling a European identity is beginning to replace the national, regional, and local identities that Europeans still cherish.

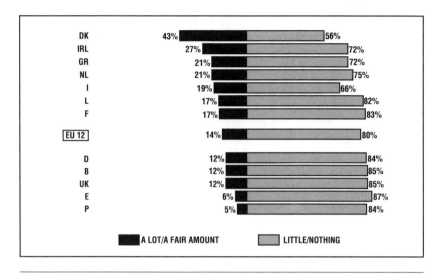

FIGURE 18A.   MAASTRICHT: HOW MUCH DO YOU KNOW?

Source: Commission of the European Communities, *Eurobarometer* (1993a).

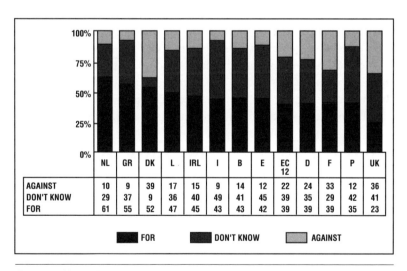

FIGURE 18B.   FOR OR AGAINST THE MAASTRICHT TREATY

Source: Commission of the European Communities, *Eurobarometer* (1993a).

If this interpretation is correct, then the conclusion may well be that as the unification process becomes more and more consequential for everyday politics, the willingness of European citizens to go along with it in their earlier casual, supportive way may be waning. However, there is probably yet another dimension to this problem. It is well known that national parliaments in the past have not been particularly interested in European politics and the decisions being taken in Brussels. As these decisions become more and more relevant, as well as controversial, for citizens—and here Maastricht is an important factor—the likelihood of policy controversies between political parties and thus the likelihood of more extensive and critical mass media reporting may also increase. Expressed in terms of electoral sociology, European unification and the EU may change from valence issues to what they at times already were in Denmark and Great Britain: position issues.

To sum up, it appears that the generous support given by EU citizens to the idea of European integration and its central actor in this process—the EU—reached a high in 1990. This is not only because, in the wake of Maastricht, the average citizen is becoming more and more aware of the implications of the process of European integration. It is also because, with Maastricht being put into effect, new elites enter the field of European action who, in the past, have given little specific consideration to European matters except for general, stereotyped support devoid of concrete content. The breakdown of socialism and of bloc politics may well be an important factor in reconsidering the European question. Therefore, the problem of transatlantic relations between Europe and the United States may command renewed attention. This final point will be elaborated next.

8. ATTITUDES TOWARD THE UNITED STATES, NATO, AND THE UNITED NATIONS

Relations between Europe and the United States mean a great many things to different people: trade, travel, cultural and scientific exchange, migration, and political relationships. In a general vein, surveys reaching back to 1954 for four leading European countries—France, Great Britain, Italy, and West Germany—speak to the fact that European mass publics on balance have become or remain emotionally attached to the United States (see table 15). This should not be taken for granted; such general attitudes often are a mixture of personal and media-created sentiments, frequently devoid of concrete political content. If one looks for a higher level of political institutionalization that might more satisfactorily reflect attachment between Western Europe and the United States, one entity immediately comes to mind: NATO.

NATO was a child and consequence of the Cold War. That attitudes in European countries toward NATO diverged substantially, depending, for

TABLE 15. WEST EUROPEAN OPINIONS OF THE UNITED STATES
1954–87

Question: "Do you have a very good, good, neither good nor bad, bad or very bad opinion of the United States?"

(Percentage favorable minus percentage unfavorable opinions)

Country	1954	1955	1956	1957	1958	1959	1960	1961
West Germany	57	56	55	58	65	65	65	71
Great Britain	40	54	51	41	52	65	49	56
Italy	49	57	65	62	53	68	57	53
France	0	17	6	4	23	31	33	42

Country	1962	1963	1964	1965	1969	1971	1972	1973
West Germany	68	75	84	73	63	51	46	45
Great Britain	52	44	66	57	41	37	49	—
Italy	61	68	74	62	52	—	60	57
France	36	36	41	28	38	32	38	—

Country	1976	1978	1981	1982	1984	1985	1987
West Germany	50	81	45	43	37	37	42
Great Britain	24	63	14	20	20	37	40
Italy	25	64	39	39	31	47	48
France	28	49	31	25	18	31	37

Sources: U.S. Information Agency surveys (1954–82); and *Eurobarometer* surveys 22, 24, 27, and 28 (the latter two surveys are combined for the 1987 results). When more than one survey was carried out in one year, the results have been averaged. Table taken from Inglehart (1990).
Note: After 1976 the category "neither good nor bad" was dropped. Thus, the absolute percentages from before and after 1976 are not comparable, but the balance between positive and negative opinions does seem to be roughly comparable across time.

example, on the share of devout communists in the country in question, therefore comes as no surprise. Obviously, there are other nation-specific factors to be taken into consideration, such as France staying out of NATO, or Greek and Spanish concerns about neighboring countries and American military bases. This, in fact, may account for the substantial regional differences that still exist in Europe regarding NATO support (table 16).

Impressive as these differences may be, they are nevertheless outweighed by the fact that—except for Greece and Spain in 1989 (a low point for pro-NATO attitudes)—in all EU member countries the majority of people consistently supported NATO, mostly by considerable margins. Given the data just alluded to, and considering that by 1991 even more people found NATO to be essential than in 1989, despite the breakdown

TABLE 16. INDEX OF COMMITMENT TO NATO BY COUNTRY (1989)

	BE	DK	FR	GE(W)	GB	GR	IR	IT	NL	PO	SP	MEAN
Very strongly pro-NATO	30	42	16	42	37	8	23	19	25	41	7	27
Strongly pro-NATO	22	25	26	21	27	16	28	20	24	28	16	23
Somewhat pro-NATO	15	8	19	8	16	13	20	18	17	10	10	14
Somewhat anti-NATO	11	6	15	6	8	10	10	13	11	6	8	9
Strongly anti-NATO	7	5	10	7	6	11	9	9	10	5	12	8
Very strongly anti-NATO	15	14	15	17	6	41	10	21	14	10	47	19
N	654	734	451	760	631	572	402	598	668	408	539	

Sources: Calculated from *Eurobarometer* no. 32 (1989). Table taken from Everts (1995).
Note: The index comprises responses to five questions about (1) a general attitude about NATO, (2) its essentiality for defense, (3) confidence in NATO decisions, (4) NATO and not EC as forum for defense decisions, and (5) acceptance of the need of U.S. military presence in Europe.

of communism and the collapse of the Soviet Union, one might be inclined to conclude that NATO, at least in principle, is alive and well.[29] On the other hand, with the decreasing emphasis on the security dimension discussed previously, the downward pressures on defense spending as a result of the economic downturn in Europe, and the ambiguous role some European members of NATO are playing in the solution of the conflict in former Yugoslavia, it may well be that public attitudes toward NATO will become more indifferent or more negative in the future. This may become the case not least because support for NATO and its goals disproportionately rests with people of rightist persuasion, the old, materialists, and less educated groups who, in the course of generational replacement, will become less of a factor in shaping and constituting public opinion in Western Europe.[30] One conclusion to be drawn therefore is that NATO as a stabilizing factor in European-U.S. relations still enjoys substantial support; this support, however, can no longer be taken for granted.

These generational considerations are not even the only reason, and very likely not the most important one, that NATO's long-term future is uncertain. The basic NATO logic of serving as a defense system against the Soviet Union and the communist bloc, which dominated thinking on security affairs in the 1950s and 1960s, had already undergone major changes by the 1970s as international elite action began to shift emphasis from confrontation to cooperation. The Soviet military intervention in Afghanistan marked a setback to these efforts. However, this period of "cold freeze" was overcome when the deployment of Pershing and cruise missiles in Western Europe in the early 1980s eventually led to formal agreements between the Soviet Union and the United States that turned out to be a major factor in the demise of communism.

Munton has shown for Germany, Canada, and Great Britain that public attitudes toward security matters are surprisingly coherent and quite responsive to changes in pertinent elite discourse and action.[31] Therefore, with respect to the public's future view of NATO, the question is whether there will be a broad national and international discourse that results in new options for NATO under once again dramatically altered circumstances.

One additional factor needs to be considered here, which was mentioned earlier. It has been argued that with the advent of the new social movements as a different type of corporate actor from established ones, the old cliché that security policy is only a matter of elite decision-making can no longer be maintained. Thomas Risse-Kappen has reiterated this insight, but has at the same time emphasized that it is also the degree of elite consensus on security matters and the policy positions of the major international actors that function as key determinants of the tides of public opinion in this field.[32] Thus, a combination of top-top, bottom-up, and top-down communication will prepare future decisions in defense and security policy.

In a more general vein, the question must be raised whether NATO is the only object of reference regarding public attitudes toward international relations. Unfortunately, the Eurobarometer surveys, to the extent they cover this topic at all, are mostly restricted to European integration and to defense policy. A factor analysis by Andrew Ziegler, Jr., based on data from the October 1980 Eurobarometer, has shown that there are indeed two dimensions to public attitudes toward international matters: the EU, and defense policy as an encompassing concept epitomized by NATO.[33] Everts has replicated Ziegler's analysis with Eurobarometer data from 1989 and 1991, and has basically corroborated Ziegler's findings of two dimensions of attitudes toward the EU and defense policy.[34] In 1989, the United Nations paid the European Commission for a series of questions about the United Nations. When these questions are included in the factor analysis, next to the two factors discussed above, the United Nations emerges as a third factor. It apparently is seen as an international actor in its own right.

If one looks first at the public visibility of the United Nations, there is no question that with 88 percent of the citizens of the EU saying they know the United Nations, this institution is highly visible. Not surprisingly, opinions on the United Nations were much more divided, with 48 percent of all EU citizens saying the United Nations is doing a good job, 39 percent saying it is doing a poor job, and 13 percent undecided.

It is also worth noting that relatively few EU citizens hold no opinion on that question. It thus appears that across Europe people are capable of looking beyond their own national affairs. This impression is also supported by the fact that when respondents were asked in an open-ended question why they felt the United Nations was doing a good or bad job, most of them could give intelligible answers.

9. CONCLUSION

This report has described and documented some of the most important sociopolitical trends in the development of the societies of Western Europe and in the orientations of their citizens. It must be emphasized again that such a task can be fulfilled only at the price of being highly selective and not penetrating deeply into various complex topics. The report is based on, and has profited from, many years of scholarly work that has produced a vast literature on the themes addressed here. It has also made use of the results of many analyses conducted by more than 60 social scientists from 15 European countries in the context of the "Beliefs in Government" project.

Undoubtedly, Western Europe after the Second World War experienced economic growth and political security for most of its citizens on a scale unparalleled in history. This situation may be attributed to the stable and thriving relations between Europe and the United States. The Marshall Plan, the Berlin air bridge, the General Agreement on Tariffs and Trade, NATO, and the growth of the EU are elements testifying to the strength of this relationship.

Underpinned by these factors, European states have been changing in many ways. The different makeup of the economy and of employment, large-scale improvements in education, the spread of modern electronic mass media, communication, and international travel have left their mark on the sociopolitical orientations of the citizenry. In related developments, the growth of political interest and involvement, redefined value and issue priorities, and a rise in mutual trust and openness between Western nations have testified to the validity of the democratic, market-inspired way of dealing with political conflict. On the other hand, people's aspirations have sometimes grown beyond realistic levels, individualism and hedonism appear to be on the rise, and dissatisfaction with the "cold project" of democracy presently seems to be more widespread than it has been for decades.

As long as the West Europeans' pursuit of happiness took place under frightful and constraining conditions of nuclear confrontation between the two superpowers, the Soviet Union and the United States, thinking about the weaknesses of Western pluralist democracies was not widespread and was further reined in by the highly visible negative example of the socialist totalitarian systems. It appears now that, with the end of the great ideological struggle between liberal democracy and communism, Western nations will have to reflect anew on their goals, their internal organization, and the role they see for themselves in a world increasingly concerned with global problems such as transnational migration, enormous population growth in some parts of the world, the transnationalization of crime, growing differences in wealth between continents, and the all-embracing challenge of threats to the environment.

Huntington's idea that the deep ideological conflicts of the past will be replaced by culturally defined tensions, particularly by those of a religious nature, may or may not have virtue.[35] Certainly, it reminds the Western Hemisphere to be mindful of the fact that the demise of communism has not done away forever with the potential for large, violent conflicts between nations or blocs of nations. The uncontrolled spread of nuclear material from the former Soviet Union will likely add a completely new and very ominous aspect to such conflicts.

The alliance between Western Europe and the United States has in the past been a cornerstone in the quest to preserve peace and democracy, at least among the OECD countries. The United States and NATO during the Cold War period found vast support from the people of Western Europe. Data presented in this report have documented that this support has not waned drastically, despite truly breathtaking changes in the political and security environment of the Alliance. While this finding is cause for satisfaction, its future validity cannot be taken for granted.

Research on people's attitudes in security matters has contributed to the common wisdom that in most situations a homogeneous stance of the national elites is the most important determinant of public opinion. This is so because individual citizens find it difficult to orient themselves in the complex field of security. Of course, the mass media have to be considered an important additional force shaping public opinion in that field, but by and large homogeneous elite positions in the past have translated into equally homogeneous public attitudes.

With changes in the political environment and the sociopolitical fabric of Western societies, elite consensus on security affairs can no longer be taken for granted. This has already had repercussions on the security orientations of the public. In addition, new systems of linkage, be they organizational or technical, and rising cognitive and operational resources in the ranks of the citizenry, have interacted with new values and new goal priorities to make the public, at least in the OECD countries, potentially much more influential and active than at any time in the past. As a result, those concerned with international relations increasingly have to consider the public at large and, in particular, specific groups, such as the new social movements, as relevant participants in national and international decision-making besides political parties and "traditional" interest groups.

Attitudes toward the EU are a case in point. As long as Brussels was a place where important and desirable things seemed to occur (which, however, did not measurably impinge on the individual citizen), elite consensus was sufficient to create and maintain a positive outlook on the EU. With the Maastricht Treaty, people in the EU began to perceive real or imminent consequences for their own lives. Movement toward a much firmer institutional link between EU members is, in addition, bringing into the picture elites that in the past displayed little interest in European affairs. Both trends, as they interact, may well explain why between 1990 and 1993 positive attitudes toward European integration and the EU have been slowly but consistently declining. These trends, however, probably also owe something to the lack of profile, visibility, and determination characteristic of public debate about the constitutional future of the European Union.

Much of this is, admittedly, speculation and interpretation. But is there also a lesson to be discerned here regarding the prospects for the transatlantic relationship? If so, it is that the task of the immediate future is to develop concrete options and related structures for this cooperation, to provide a forum for public debate, and then to find public support for whatever options best serve the interests of those involved in maintaining and strengthening the transatlantic relationship.

A final consideration: electoral research has shown that over the last two decades voter alignments with established parties have been on the wane. One consequence of this is growing voter volatility. This argument can be turned around by pointing to the decreasing capacity of established corporate actors to find reliable backing from their clientele for their policies and decisions. As a result, the national and international process becomes more difficult to manage, and outcomes become less calculable. These are changes resulting from shifts in the political orientation of citizens that cannot be undone, except perhaps temporarily in times of grave crisis.

NOTES

1. Daniel Bell, *The Coming of Post-Industrial Society* (London: Heinemann, 1974).
2. Zbigniew Brzezinski, *Macht und Moral: Neue Werte Für die Weltpolitik* (Hamburg: Hoffmann und Campe, 1994).
3. One noteworthy example in Germany is a series of publications by the *Allensbach Institut für Demoskopie*, directed by Elisabeth Noelle-Neumann.

In 1993 the institute presented its most recent volume (no. 9) of its "Allensbacher Jahrbuch der Demoskopie, 1984–1992." Also, the regular surveys by the Social Community Planning Research Institute in the United Kingdom, which are published in the British Social Attitudes reports, deserve mention.

4. William Kornhauser, *The Politics of Mass Society* (New York: Free Press, 1959).

5. Stefano Bartolini and Peter Mair, *Identity, Competition and Electoral Availability: The Stabilization of European Electorates, 1885–1985* (Cambridge: Cambridge University Press, 1990).

6. For details, see Ferdinand Müller-Rommel, *Grüne Parteien in Westeuropa: Entwicklungsphasen und Erfolgsbedingungen* (Opladen: Westdeutscher Verlag, 1993).

7. Ronald Inglehart, *Culture Shift in Advanced Industrial Society* (Princeton: Princeton University Press, 1990).

8. See Ivor Crewe and David Denver, eds., *Electoral Change in Western Democracies: Patterns and Sources of Electoral Volatility* (London: Croom Helm, 1985); Russell J. Dalton, Scott H. Flanagan, and Paul Allen Beck, eds., *Electoral Change in Advanced Industrial Democracies: Realignment or Dealignment?* (Princeton: Princeton University Press, 1984); and Russell J. Dalton and Robert Rohrschneider, "Wählerwandel und die Abschwächung der Parteineigung von 1972 bis 1987," in *Wahlen und Wähler. Analysen aus Anlaß der Bundestagswahl 1987*, Max Kaase and Hans-Dieter Klingemann, eds. (Opladen: Westdeutscher Verlag, 1990), pp. 297–324.

9. For some preliminary analyses, see Thomas Poguntke, "Anti-Party Sentiment. Conceptual Thoughts and Empirical Evidence: Explorations into a Minefield." *European Journal of Political Research* 29: special issue, "The Politics of Party Sentiment," Thomas Poguntke and Susan E. Scarrow, eds., (forthcoming).

10. Hanspeter Kriesi, *Political Mobilization and Social Change: The Dutch Case in Comparative Perspective* (Aldershot: Avebury, 1993).

11. Ronald Inglehart, "The Silent Revolution in Europe: Intergenerational Change in Post-Industrial Societies," *American Political Science Review* 65 (1971), pp. 991–1017.

12. See Inglehart, *Culture Shift in Advanced Industrial Society*.

13. See Ronald Inglehart and Paul R. Abramson, "Economic Security and Value Change," *American Political Science Review* 88 (1994) p. 342.

14. Ibid., p. 349.

15. Klaus R. Allerbeck, *Demokratisierung und sozialer Wandel in der Bundesrepublik Deutschland: Sekundäranalyse von Umfragedaten, 1953–1974* (Opladen: Westdeutscher Verlag, 1976).

16. See Elisabeth Noelle-Neumann and Renate Köcher, *Die verletzte Nation: Über den Versuch der Deutschen, ihren Charakter zu ändern* (Stuttgart: Deutsche Verlags-Anstalt, 1987), pp. 164–281. See also Inglehart, *Culture Shift in Advanced Industrial Society*, p. 177–211.

17. Helmut Klages, *Wertedynamik: Über die Wandelbarkeit des Selbstverständlichen.* Texte und Thesen, Band 212 (Zürich: Edition Interfrom, 1988).
18. See Müller-Rommel, *Grüne Parteien in Westeuropa: Entwick lungsphasen und Erfolgsbedingungen*, pp. 170–71.
19. Max Kaase, "Direct Political Participation in the Late Eighties in the EU Countries," in Peter Gundelach and Karen Siune, eds., *From Voters to Participants*, (Aarhus: Politica, 1992), pp. 75–90.
20. Arthur H. Miller, "Political Issues and Trust in Government: 1964–1970," *American Political Science Review* 68 (1974), pp. 951–72.
21. Paul M. Sniderman, *A Question of Loyalty* (Berkeley: University of California Press, 1981).
22. Bettina Westle, *Politische Legitimität—Theorien, Konzepte, empirische Befunde* (Baden-Baden: Nomos, 1989).
23. David Easton, *A Systems Analysis of Political Life* (New York: John Wiley, 1965).
24. Dieter Fuchs, Giovanna Guidorossi, and Palle Svensson, "Support for the Democratic System," in Hans-Dieter Klingemann and Dieter Fuchs, eds., *Citizens and State*, Beliefs in Government Series, vol. 1. (Oxford: Oxford University Press, 1995), pp. 323–53.
25. This is empirically demonstrated by Everts and Sinnott, "NATO, The European Community, and the United Nations," pp. 419–20.
26. Oskar Niedermayer, "Trends and Contrasts," in Oskar Niedermayer and Richard Sinnott, eds., *Public Opinion and Internationalized Governance*, Beliefs in Government Series, vol. 2. (Oxford: Oxford University Press, 1995), pp. 53–72.
27. Commission of the European Communities, "Public Opinion in the European Community," in *Eurobarometer* 39, June 1993 (Brussels: Commission of the European Communities, 1993), pp. 70, 88, 97, 113.
28. Niedermayer, "Support for European Integration: Trends and Contrasts."
29. Philip H. Everts and Richard Sinnott, "Conclusion: European Publics and the Legitimacy of Internationalized Governance," in Oskar Niedermayer and Richard Sinnott, eds., *Public Opinion and Internationalized Governance*, pp. 431–57.
30. See also Inglehart, *Culture Shift in Advanced Industrial Society*, pp. 414–17.
31. Don Munton, "NATO against the Wall: Changing Security Attitudes in Germany, Britain and Canada, 1960s to 1980s," in Hans Rattinger and Don Munton, eds. , *Debating National Security: The Public Dimension*, (Frankfurt am Main: Peter Lang, 1991), pp. 343–77.
32. Thomas Risse-Kappen, "Anti-Nuclear and Pro-Détente? The Transformation of the West German Security Debate," in Hans Rattinger and Don Munton, eds., *Debating National Security: The Public Dimension*, (Frankfurt am Main: Peter Lang, 1991), pp. 269–99.

33. Andrew H. Ziegler, Jr., "The Structure of Western European Attitudes towards Atlantic Cooperation: Implications for the Western Alliance," *British Journal of Political Science* 17 (1987), pp. 457–77.
34. Everts "NATO, the European Community, and the United Nations."
35. Samuel P. Huntington, "The Clash of Civilizations? The Next Pattern of Conflict," *Foreign Affairs* 72(1993), pp. 22–49.

BIBLIOGRAPHY

Aarts, Kees. "Linkage and Responsibility: Intermediate Organizations and Interest Representation." In *Citizens and the State*, edited by Hans-Dieter Klingemann and Dieter Fuchs, 227–57. Beliefs in Government Series, vol. 1. Oxford: Oxford University Press, 1995.

Allerbeck, Klaus R. *Demokratisierung und sozialer Wandel in der Bundesrepublik Deutschland: Sekundäranalyse von Umfragedaten, 1953–1974*. Opladen: Westdeutscher Verlag, 1976.

Almond, Gabriel A., and Sidney Verba. *The Civic Culture*. Princeton: Princeton University Press, 1963.

Bartolini, Stefano, and Peter Mair. *Identity, Competition and Electoral Availability: The Stabilization of European Electorates 1885–1985*. Cambridge: Cambridge University Press, 1990.

Bell, Daniel. *The Coming of Post-Industrial Society*. London: Heinemann, 1974.

Brzezinski, Zbigniew. 1994. *Macht und Moral: Neue Werte für die Weltpolitik*. Hamburg: Hoffmann und Campe, 1994.

Commission of the European Communities (1993a). "Public Opinion in the European Community." In *Eurobarometer* 39, June 1993. Brussels: Commission of the European Communities.

Commission of the European Communities (1993b). *Eurobarometer: Trends 1974–1992*. Brussels: Commission of the European Communities, 1993.

Crewe, Ivor, and David Denver, eds. *Electoral Change in Western Democracies: Patterns and Sources of Electoral Volatility*. London: Croom Helm, 1985.

Dalton, Russell J., Scott H. Flanagan, and Paul Allen Beck, eds. *Electoral Change in Advanced Industrial Democracies: Realignment or Dealignment*. Princeton: Princeton University Press, 1984.

Dalton, Russell J., and Robert Rohrschneider. "Wählerwandel und die Abschwächung der Parteieneigung von 1972 bis 1987." In *Wahlen und Wähler: Analysen aus Anlass der Bundestagswahl 1987*, edited by Max Kaase and Hans-Dieter Klingemann, 297–324. Opladen: Westdeutscher Verlag, 1990.

van Deth, Jan W. "A Macro-Setting for Micro-Politics." In *The Impact of Values*, edited by Jan W. van Deth and Elinor Scarbrough, 48–75. Beliefs in Government Series, vol. 4. Oxford: Oxford University Press, 1995.

Easton, David. *A Systems Analysis of Political Life*. New York: John Wiley, 1965.

European Comission."Public Opinion in the European Union." In *Eurobarometer* 40, December 1993.

Everts, Philip P. "NATO, the European Community and the United Nations." In *The Internationalization of Governance*, edited by Oskar Niedermayer and Richard Sinnott, 402–28. Beliefs in Government Series, vol. 2. Oxford: Oxford University Press.

Everts, Philip H. and Richard Sinnott. "Conclusion: European Publics and the Legitimacy of Internationalized Governance." In *The Internationalization of Governance*, edited by Oskar Niedermayer and Richard Sinnott, 431–57. Beliefs in Government Series, vol. 2. Oxford: Oxford University Press, 1995.

Fuchs, Dieter, and Dieter Rucht. "Support for New Social Movements in Five Western European Countries." In *Social Change and Political Transformation*, edited by Chris Rootes and Howard Davis, 86–110. London: UCL Press Limited, 1994.

Fuchs, Dieter, Giovanna Guidorossi, and Palle Svensson. "Support for the Democratic System." In *Citizens and the State*, edited by Hans-Dieter Klingemann and Dieter Fuchs, 323–53. Beliefs in Government Series, vol. 1. Oxford: Oxford University Press, 1995.

Huntington, Samuel P. "The Clash of Civilizations? The Next Pattern of Conflict." *Foreign Affairs* 72 (1993): 22–49.

Inglehart, Ronald. "The Silent Revolution in Europe: Intergenerational Change in Post-Industrial Societies." *American Political Science Review* 65(1971): 991–1017.

Inglehart, Ronald. *Culture Shift in Advanced Industrial Society*. Princeton: Princeton University Press, 1990.

Inglehart, Ronald, and Paul R. Abramson. "Economic Security and Value Change." *American Political Science Review* 88 (1994): 336–54.

Jagodzinski, Wolfgang and Karel Dobbelaere. "Secularization and Church Religiosity." In *The Impact of Values*, edited by Jan W. van Deth and Elinor Scarbrough, 76–119. Beliefs in Government Series, vol. 4. Oxford: Oxford University Press, 1995.

Kaase, Max. "Direct Political Participation in the Late Eighties in the EU Countries." In *From Voters to Participants*, edited by Peter Gundelach and Karen Siune, 75–90. Aarhus: Politica, 1992.

Katz, Richard, and Peter Mair, eds. "The Membership in Political Parties in European Democracies, 1960–1990." *European Journal of Political Research* 22, no. 3, 1992.

Katz, Richard, and Peter Mair, eds. *The Development of Party Organizations in Western Democracies, 1966–1990: A Data Handbook*. London: Sage Publications, 1992.

Klages, Helmut. *Wertedynamik: Über die Wandelbarkeit des Selbstverständlichen*. Texte und Thesen, Band 212. Zürich: Edition Interfrom, 1988.

Klingemann, Hans-Dieter and Dieter Fuchs, eds. *Citizens and the State*. Beliefs in Government Series, vol. 1. Oxford: Oxford University Press, 1995.

Kornhauser, William. *The Politics of Mass Society*. New York: Free Press, 1959.

Kriesi, Hanspeter. *Political Mobilization and Social Change: The Dutch Case in Comparative Perspective*. Aldershot: Avebury, 1993.

Lane, Jan-Erik, David McKay and Kenneth Newton. *Political Data Handbook: OECD Countries*. Oxford: Oxford University Press, 1991.

Miller, Arthur H. "Political Issues and Trust in Government: 1964–1970." *American Political Science Review* 68 (1974): 951–72.

Müller-Rommel, Ferdinand. *Grüne Parteien in Westeuropa: Entwicklungsphasen und Erfolgsbedingungen*. Opladen: Westdeutscher Verlag, 1993.

Munton, Don. "NATO against the Wall: Changing Security Attitudes in Germany, Britain and Canada, 1960s to 1980s." In *Debating National Security: The Public Dimension*, edited by Hans Rattinger and Don Munton, 343–77. Frankfurt am Main: Peter Lang, 1991.

Niedermayer, Oskar. "Trends and Contrasts." In *The Internationalization of Governance*, edited by Oskar Niedermayer and Richard Sinnott, 53–72. Beliefs in Government Series, vol. 2. Oxford: Oxford University Press, 1995.

Noelle-Neumann, Elisabeth and Renate Köcher. *Die verletzte Nation: Über den Versuch der Deutschen, ihren Charakter zu ändern*. Stuttgart: Deutsche Verlags-Anstalt, 1987.

Poguntke, Thomas. "Anti-Party Sentiment. Conceptual Thoughts and Empirical Evidence: Explorations into a Minefield." In *European Journal of Political Research* 29, special issue, "The Politics of Party Sentiment," edited by Thomas Poguntke and Susan E. Scarrow (forthcoming).

Risse-Kappen, Thomas. "Anti-Nuclear and Pro-Détente? The Transformation of the West German Security Debate." In *Debating National Security: The Public Dimension*, edited by Hans Rattinger and Don Munton, 269–99. Frankfurt am Main: Peter Lang, 1991.

Roller, Edeltraut. "Political Agendas and Beliefs About the Scope of Government." In *The Scope of Government*, edited by Ole Borre and Elinor Scarbrough, 55–86. Beliefs in Government Series, vol. 3. Oxford: Oxford University Press, 1995.

Schmitt, Hermann and Sören Holmberg. "Political Parties in Decline?" In *Citizens and the State*, edited by Hans-Dieter Klingemann and Dieter Fuchs, 95–133. Beliefs in Government Series, vol. 1. Oxford: Oxford University Press, 1995.

Sniderman, Paul M. *A Question of Loyalty*. Berkeley: University of California Press, 1981.

Topf, Richard. "Beyond Electoral Participation." In *Citizens and the State*, edited by Hans-Dieter Klingemann and Dieter Fuchs, 52–92. Beliefs in Government Series, vol. 1. Oxford: Oxford University Press, 1995.

Visser, Jelle. *European Trade Unions in Figures*. Deventer: Kluwer, 1989.

Westle, Bettina. *Politische Legitimität—Theorien, Konzepte, empirische Befunde*. Baden-Baden: Nomos, 1989.

Widfeldt, Anders. "Party Membership and Party Representativeness" In *Citizens and the State*, edited by Hans-Dieter Klingemann and Dieter Fuchs,134–82. Beliefs in Government Series, vol. 1. Oxford: Oxford University Press, 1995.

Ziegler, Jr., Andrew H. "The Structure of Western European Attitudes towards Atlantic Cooperation: Implications for the Western Alliance." *British Journal of Political Science* 17 (1987): 457–77.

Societal Change in the United States and Its Transatlantic Consequences from an Empirical Perspective

Andrew Kohut

1. INTRODUCTION

The end of the Cold War marked the beginning of an epoch of confusion, apprehension, and dissension about the role of the United States in a new world order. Reeling from the rapid sequence of events that has transformed world politics, America finds itself in the midst of a foreign policy identity crisis. The core values that had driven international affairs for decades are no longer appropriate. Without the communist threat around which to organize an agenda, America's leaders are uncertain about their country's place in the world. It is not even clear that they are searching hard for new principles to guide U.S. foreign policy in the post-Soviet world.

The public's current disposition adds much to America's disarray in foreign affairs. The U.S. public is contentious, self-absorbed, and at the same time politically energized. Almost to the point of ignoring the rest of the world, Americans are seriously concerned about challenges at home, especially economic recovery, health care, and crime. In the public's view, foreign policy should serve the U.S. domestic program, and global issues should be treated according to their impact on national affairs.

According to a 1993 study by the Times Mirror Center for the People and the Press about America's place in the post–Cold War world, elites also emphasize domestic concerns when considering foreign policy goals and priorities.[1] While they shun old-fashioned isolationism, they advocate an internationalism that is cautious and minimalist. They see no single global mission for America in the world today. American opinion leaders are united mainly in believing that the nation should be chary about exporting its long-standing moral values of democracy, human rights, self-determination, and capitalism.

This essay explores trends in American attitudes, values, and behavior that coincide with both momentous and more subtle political and cultural transformations in society. Using extensive survey data, it examines how both elites and average citizens feel about America's place in the world today. Since Americans are strongly inclined to view foreign policy through domestic lenses, it will also examine citizens' political values and attitudes toward their own institutions. These attitudes will be explored within the context of the cultural and generational bases of change in the United States, focusing especially on the information and technology revolutions that are currently in high gear. In so doing, the report will provide insights into how Americans perceive their relationships abroad.

2. AMERICA'S ROLE IN THE POST–COLD WAR WORLD

The Times Mirror Center report entitled "America's Place in the New World" reveals that elite and public opinion about foreign affairs is decidedly more complex now than it was in the Cold War period. The study is based upon a survey of the nation's top leaders—American "influentials"—from nine domains (media, business and finance, entertainment and culture, foreign affairs, security, state and local government, think tanks and academia, religion, and science and engineering) and a parallel poll of the general public. The report compares where these two groups believe America stands today, on both domestic and foreign affairs issues, and where they think the country should be headed.[2]

Specifically, the influentials and average citizens were asked to address the following concerns: What are the most important problems facing the United States? What are the greatest foreign dangers? What should America's top goals be in economic, political, security, and ecological realms? What leadership role should the United States play in a new world order? What are America's top policy priorities? And which area of the world is now most important to America—the Pacific Rim or Europe?

Generally speaking, American influentials are not celebrating the end of the Cold War. They are not optimistic about the way things are going in either the United States or the world today. Elites are troubled as they see former communist states move toward authoritarian political organization, or outright ethnic warfare, instead of toward the liberal, pluralist democracies of the West.

Influentials differ profoundly among themselves about the nature of the problems confronting America in the new world. They are even more divided when it comes to assigning priority to the problems. There is, however, a dual imperative running through elites' responses: maintain peace and serve the domestic agenda through foreign policy. Influentials champion peace over intervention. They advocate protecting the global environment and strengthening the United Nations over promoting democracy and human rights abroad. Fortifying the domestic economy is considered by all influential groups to be the policy priority requiring the greatest attention.

In September 1993 the general public was even more pessimistic than were elites about the country's future. A remarkable finding of the study is that 75 percent of Americans are dissatisfied with the way things are going in the United States, whereas 66 percent are unhappy with the way things are going in the world. Figure 1 compares the influentials' and the public's levels of dissatisfaction with the way things are going in the United States and in the world.[3]

The general public insists that domestic concerns should receive even higher priority than elites would give them. Citizens consider most important those international problems that pose a threat to their personal and economic security, or that threaten their lifestyles, such as drug trafficking.

Even pivotal world events, such as the political transformations in Eastern and Central Europe following the end of the Cold War, including the reunification of Germany, and the struggle to stop oppression in South Africa, fail to engage the majority of American citizens. The huge gap between the public's concern with domestic issues and with international issues is illustrated by the findings of a Times Mirror Center study conducted during the week of the landmark peace accords between Israel and the Palestine Liberation Organization in September 1993. Only 19 percent of the public followed the peace accords closely in the news, while 37 percent paid close attention to the prospects for the Clinton administration's health care reform. Many similar contrasts are found in Times Mirror monthly News Interest Index reports.

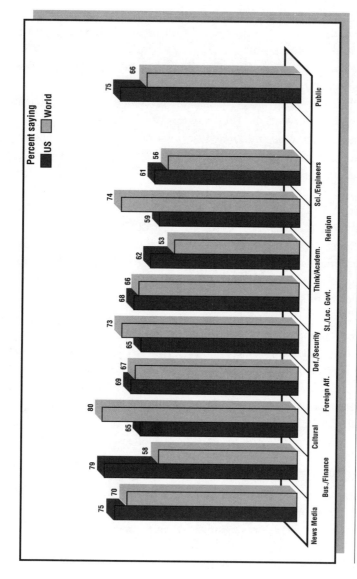

FIGURE 1. DISSATISFACTION WITH CONDITIONS IN THE UNITED STATES VERSUS THE WORLD

Source: Times Mirror Center for the People and the Press, *America's Place in the World: An Investigation of the Attitudes of American Opinion Leaders and the American Public about International Affairs* (Washington, D.C.: Times Mirror Center for the People and the Press, 1993).

Greatest Foreign Dangers

Atheistic communism, embodied in an expansionist Soviet Union, once represented a single enemy to virtually all nine of the nation's leadership groups included in the study. Today, American elites are far from united on the main dangers facing their country, whether these are posed in terms of individual nations, ideology, or ecology.

The complexities of the new international order render it more difficult now than in the past for elites to evaluate and to act on the challenges that lie ahead. The overriding threat of the Cold War—a nuclear conflict—provides an example of how influentials view dangers on the international front. On the one hand, influentials feel that the threat of global catastrophe is reduced now that the Soviet Union no longer exists. However, that threat has been replaced by the danger of nuclear weapons proliferation. Yet the threat of nuclear holocaust is not the primary concern of the nation's leaders.

Asked about the greatest threat to world stability, many influentials ranked nationalism and ethnic hatred highest on their list of concerns. Population growth and weapons proliferation vied for second place, followed by religious fanaticism.

Most Americans believed that nationalism/ethnic hatred and nuclear proliferation, respectively, pose the greatest threats to international harmony. Departing markedly from influentials, they ranked the issue of environmental pollution—a problem found as much at home as abroad—a strong third. Population growth and religious fanaticism were of much less concern. Influentials and the general public's ratings of the greatest dangers to world stability appear in table 1.

As table 2 demonstrates, most of the influentials felt that among potential events affecting peace and stability by the end of the century, the emergence of China as an assertive global power was most probable. A distant second in this respect was the possibility that Germany might dominate Europe politically and economically. However, elites seemed generally unconcerned about these anticipated events. Indeed, they flatly dismissed the idea of guarding against a resurgent Germany. Very few influentials saw the need for the United States to be more vigilant toward the emergence of Beijing on the world scene. A majority opposed giving a greater military role to Japan, which is an obvious military hedge against China as well as Germany.

TABLE 1. PERCENTAGE OF RESPONDENTS BY ISSUE THEY CONSIDER THE GREATEST DANGER TO WORLD STABILITY

First Choices	Media	Business	Cultural	Foreign Affairs	Security	State/Local Govt.	Academics	Religion	Sci./ Eng.	Genl. Public
Nationalism and ethnic hatreds	47	33	24	33	44	35	49	40	15	27
Proliferation of weapons of mass destruction	18	22	13	39	35	19	17	26	14	24
International trade conflicts	4	12	1	*	3	17	4	2	2	7
Religious fanaticism	15	20	15	6	3	12	9	11	16	11
Environmental pollution	3	1	15	*	4	1	*	11	1	18
Population growth	14	12	29	22	7	14	18	11	51	10

Source: Times Mirror Center for the People and the Press, *America's Place in the World.*

TABLE 2. INFLUENTIALS' FORECAST OF WORLD EVENTS (TOP FIVE "CERTAIN" PLUS "PROBABLE" MENTIONS)

	1	2	3	4	5
Media	China emerges	Germany dominates	Int'l terrorism in U.S. rises	Western Europe unifies	Jap. economic power wanes
Business	China emerges	Germany dominates	Jap. economic* power wanes	Iran-Iraq war resumes	Israeli-Arab war resumes
Foreign Affairs	China emerges	Germany dominates	N. Korean communism ends	Int'l terrorism in U.S. rises*	Iran-Iraq war resumes
Security	China emerges	Germany dominates	N. Korean communism ends	China uses force*	Russia retakes empire
State/Local Govt.	China emerges	Int'l terrorism in U.S. rises	Western Europe unifies	Germany dominates*	Iran-Iraq war resumes
Religion	China emerges	Int'l terrorism in U.S. rises	Germany dominates*	Jap. economic power wanes	Iran-Iraq war resumes

*Indicates this item is tied with the following item for this particular group.
Source: Times Mirror Center for the People and the Press, *America's Place in the World.*

When asked to select which country, if any, represents the greatest danger to the United States, influentials held widely diverse opinions (see table 3). Iran was the favorite overall, although fewer than one in seven named it. There were major differences among specific groups of influentials. A quarter of the foreign affairs elite cited Iran. The security group mostly chose China, along with Russia and the other former Soviet states. The media chose Iraq, while the business group pointed at Japan—presumably as an economic threat rather than a political or military danger.

America's Top Foreign Policy Goals

All nine influential groups agreed that the top foreign policy goal for the country is the prevention of the spread of weapons of mass destruction. More than 80 percent of those surveyed felt this was the first priority. Ensuring adequate energy supplies for the country came in a distant second place. These were the only universally shared foreign policy objectives observed in the Times Mirror study. Other objectives that were ranked high on the influentials' list included improving the global environment, reducing the foreign trade deficit, protecting American jobs, and strengthening the United Nations.

The general public differed greatly from elites in assessing America's top foreign policy goals. Average citizens overwhelmingly chose protecting American jobs (85 percent) as the most important foreign policy goal. Nuclear proliferation was a distant second (69 percent), followed by ensuring energy supplies, protecting the environment, and reducing trade deficits.[4] The top five foreign policy goals for influentials and the general public appear in figure 2.

One of the most significant findings of this study is that influential Americans feel that the United States should abandon its policy of exporting Western democratic values and principles to the rest of the world, especially if such a policy "seriously risks" undesirable consequences. Most support came for promoting democracy in precarious circumstances, but this was nonetheless a minority view. Leaders were also vehemently against—by a margin of two to one—urging the United States to apply its human and civil rights standards abroad if that seriously risked antagonizing friendly nations whose traditions are different from Western ideals.

TABLE 3. PERCENTAGE OF RESPONDENTS BY COUNTRY THEY CONSIDER THE GREATEST DANGER TO THE UNITED STATES

	Media	Business	Cultural	Foreign Affairs	Security	State/ Local Govt.	Academics	Religion	Sci. Eng.
ASIA									
China	9	9	10	10	21	12	17	9	12
Japan	9	14	11	7	9	13	10	6	10
North Korea	4	1	5	*	1	4	1	*	1
MIDDLE EAST									
Iran	13	10	13	25	15	7	8	13	19
Iraq	15	12	10	9	3	17	10	15	11
Middle East countries	3	1	4	*	*	4	6	9	1
Other Middle East mentions	1	*	3	1	*	1	1	*	1
FORMER SOVIET UNION									
Former Soviet Union	4	12	3	7	6	6	8	*	5
Russia	4	6	*	6	16	4	5	*	2
Ukraine	1	3	*	1	1	*	*	*	*

Source: Times Mirror Center for the People and the Press, *America's Place in the World.*

News Media
Preventing spread of nuclear weapons
Insuring adequate energy supplies
Improving global environment
Protecting jobs of American workers
Reducing trade deficit

State/Local Government
Preventing spread of nuclear weapons
Insuring adequate energy supplies
Reducing trade deficit
Protecting jobs of American workers
Improving global environment

Business/Finance
Preventing spread of nuclear weapons
Insuring adequate energy supplies
Reducing trade deficit
Aiding interests of U.S. business abroad
Protecting jobs of American workers

Think Tanks/Academics
Preventing spread of nuclear weapons
Insuring adequate energy supplies
Improving global environment
Reducing trade deficit
Strengthening the U.N.

Cultural
Preventing spread of nuclear weapons
Improving global environment
Insuring adequate energy supplies
Protecting jobs of American workers
Strengthening the U.N.

Religion
Preventing spread of nuclear weapons
Insuring adequate energy supplies
Promoting/defending human rights
Protecting jobs of American workers
Reducing trade deficit

Foreign Affairs
Preventing spread of nuclear weapons
Insuring adequate energy supplies
Strengthening the U.N.
Improving global environment
Reducing trade deficit

Science/Engineering
Preventing spread of nuclear weapons
Improving global environment
Insuring adequate energy supplies
Reducing trade deficit
Strengthening the U.N.

Security
Preventing spread of nuclear weapons
Insuring adequate energy supplies
Strengthening the U.N.
Promoting democracy
Improving global environment

General Public
Protecting jobs of American workers
Preventing spread of nuclear weapons
Insuring adequate energy supplies
Improving global environment
Reducing trade deficit

FIGURE 2. TOP FIVE FOREIGN POLICY GOALS

Source: Times Mirror Center for the People and the Press, *America's Place in the World.*

Influentials were markedly unwilling to promote free markets and economic capitalism if the outcome meant exploitation of underdeveloped peoples by Western businessmen. Finally, with an obvious eye on Bosnia and Yugoslavia, nine out of ten influentials opposed promoting self-determination of ethnic groups if it risked creating warring factions out of established nations.

The public was more opposed than the influentials to promoting most of these values when the United States faced the potential of a risky outcome, with one exception. Some 15 percent of average citizens said it was worth the risk to promote self-determination. Support for this proposition among the public was twice the level expressed by the influentials.

Table 4 provides a comparison of elites and the public on their willingness to export Western ideals abroad.[5]

However leery of promoting principles abroad, the influentials were clearly prepared to send American fighting men to honor long-standing U.S. commitments and to protect vital interests. By margins of about two-thirds or more, they would support the use of American forces to defend Saudi Arabia against Iraq, South Korea against North Korea, and Israel against Arab invaders.

In contrast to influentials, according to the June 1995 survey, the public appeared willing to go to war for almost no country other than the United States itself. The exception was to fight Iraq (53 percent in favor, 40 percent against), presumably to secure oil supplies and to protect the

TABLE 4. PERCENTAGE OF RESPONDENTS WILLING
TO EXPORT WESTERN IDEALS

	Promote Democracy*	Human Rights†	Ethnic Self-Determination‡	Economic Capitalism§
News Media	48	35	4	27
Business/Finance	32	6	—	57
Cultural	34	34	9	18
Foreign Affairs	49	33	3	36
Defense/Security	49	31	4	44
State/Local Government	36	22	14	30
Think Tanks/ Academia	44	38	8	44
Religion	40	45	9	9
Science/Engineers	44	37	4	30
General Public	30	26	15	18

Source: Times Mirror Center for the People and the Press, *America's Place in the World.*
*Even if it seriously risks the election of totalitarian and anti-American governments.
†Even if it seriously risks antagonizing friendly nations whose historical, cultural, and religious traditions do not conform to Western ideals.
‡Even if it seriously risks leading to the the break-up of those nations into warring ethnic regions.
§Even if it seriously risks exploitation of underdeveloped peoples by Western businessmen.

Gulf War victory. American citizens were strongly against fighting on behalf of South Korea (63 percent versus 31 percent), and marginally against fighting for Israel (52 percent versus 41 percent).[6]

A majority of the influentials favored placing American troops in a permanent force under U.N. command. However, the public was very unsympathetic to the idea. Opposition ran considerably more than two to one against (69 percent versus 25 percent) among average citizens. These results were obtained prior to the death of American rangers in Somalia. Table 5 displays the findings for support of U.S. forces serving abroad.

Defense

A solid majority of six in ten influentials favored deeper cuts in defense spending than the Clinton administration has proposed, although almost one-third of respondents opposed further reductions. The public, surprisingly, is strongly in favor of keeping defense spending as it is (52 percent) or increasing it (10 percent).[7]

TABLE 5.   PERCENTAGE OF RESPONDENTS WHO WOULD APPROVE
OF THE USE OF U.S. FORCES ABROAD

	Iraq/ Saudi Arabia*	North Korea/ South Korea†	U.S. Forces/ U.N. Command‡
News Media	74	69	71
Business/Finance	87	72	51
Cultural	58	43	74
Foreign Affairs	93	86	77
Defense/Security	92	92	72
State/Local Government	73	65	57
Think Tanks/Academia	83	77	80
Religion	55	49	75
Science/Engineers	69	68	77
General Public	53	31	25

Source: Times Mirror Center for the People and the Press, America's Place in the World.
*If Iraq invaded Saudi Arabia.
†If North Korea invaded South Korea.
‡American forces serving under U.N. command.

Almost half of the influentials would keep U.S. troop strength in Europe at the 100,000-troop level now planned for the future (down from 300,000 in Cold War days). More than one-third of influentials would cut forces to significantly below the 100,000-person level, however, and more than one in ten favor bringing the U.S. force home entirely. In contrast, a two-thirds majority of influentials would favor keeping U.S. troop strength in South Korea as it is, at 39,000, with fewer than one in four in favor of deep cuts and fewer than one in ten in favor of bringing all the troops home.

There is overwhelming support among influentials (90 percent overall) for negotiating further cuts in the U.S. nuclear arsenal from the 3,500-weapon ceiling due to be reached in the year 2003 under agreements already signed. Most favor a level of 1,500 strategic weapons or fewer, compared with roughly 12,000 weapons at the height of the Cold War.

Most Important Nations

By a small margin, the influentials feel that Japan and the Pacific Rim countries are now marginally more important to the United States than Europe is. Of those who chose Europe, four out of ten cited mainly cultural and ethnic reasons, with political and economic matters receiving only minor mentions. More than three-fourths of those selecting the Pacific Rim volunteered economic reasons for their choice. Security concerns were seldom mentioned by influentials as a reason for their focus on Asia, even though the United States has fought three wars there in the last half century. However, elites considered Asian nations—China, Japan, and North Korea—to be more dangerous to the United States than the nations of Europe, including Russia and the former Soviet states.

Europe is still number one with the public, however. Fully one-half identified the Continent as being most important, while fewer than one-third chose Asia. Only eight percent felt that the two were equally consequential. Figure 3 compares influentials' and the public's assessments of the part of the world that is most important to the United States.

Trade Relationships

While influentials may see Asia as representing a more important player than Europe in relation to the United States, they recognize a good deal

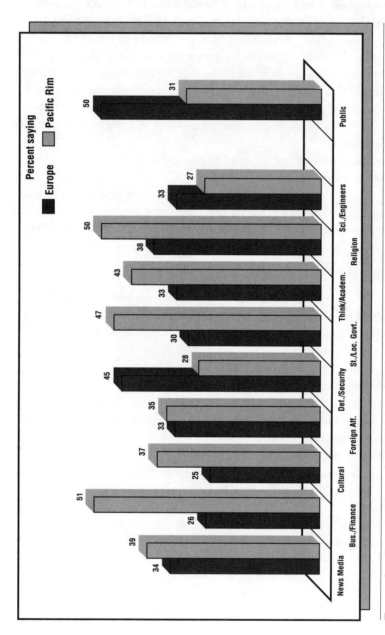

FIGURE 3. PART OF WORLD MOST IMPORTANT TO THE UNITED STATES

Source: Times Mirror Center for the People and the Press, *America's Place in the World.*

of tension in that relationship. More than eight in ten influentials feel that Japan is an unfair trading partner with America.

There was far greater satisfaction among influentials with the European Community as a trading partner than there was with Japan. A minority—one in three—labeled the EC as unfair, while nearly half considered it fair. There were significant group differences among the elites. A majority of respondents in the business, foreign affairs, and security groups (51 percent, 48 percent, and 48 percent, respectively) felt that the European Community was unfair in trade relations. However, there was little support for retaliation against Japan or Europe within any group (7 percent for, 27 percent against).

There are big gaps in elite and public opinion on the issue of the North American Free Trade Agreement. Support for NAFTA is overwhelming among all influentials. Well over 80 percent of the elite survey respondents were in favor of the agreement. Average Americans, however, are more skeptical. A Times Mirror poll conducted in October reveals that the plan is backed by only 46 percent of the public, while there was far less support for NAFTA among elements of the public that paid the most attention to the debate on this subject.[8] The informed public was divided 42 percent in favor, 37 percent opposed.[9]

U.S. Role in a New World Order

Influentials are uncertain and somewhat pessimistic about America's authority in the world today and its ability to influence global events. Approximately one-third of elite respondents believed that the United States plays a less important role in world affairs now than it did a decade ago. A majority of the security group felt America has less clout now (54 percent), with the business group close behind (49 percent). Only one in four influentials believed that the country is more important now, while one-third thought it was just as important as it was ten years ago.

The public's perception of America's standing in the new world order is not nearly as bleak as that of the influentials. Some 37 percent of citizens believed that the United States is playing a more powerful role today than yesterday, 30 percent considered it less important, and 31 percent felt that the U.S. position has remained unchanged.[10]

While the United States remains the dominant military power in the eyes of influentials, only a small minority of them want the country to be the world's single leader. With the huge cost of America's leadership in the Cold War now apparent, most elites want Washington to share leadership with others. At the same time, they are reluctant to see the passing of U.S. dominance. A majority of influentials feel that America should be the most assertive nation at the top table, even as it shares power with other countries. There is little support within this group for America's becoming less assertive in its world leadership role. In fact, more than two-thirds of the influentials want the United States to be either the world's single leader or its preeminent leader, what Paul Nitze has termed its "preponderant power."

While the vast majority of influentials preferred a shared leadership role for the United States, there were vast differences among the groups about what kind of shared role was best. Support for the most assertive option was found heavily among the government (77 percent) and foreign affairs (68 percent) groups. This option was also favored more by men than by women (60 percent and 44 percent, respectively—not shown). The nonassertive option received its strongest endorsement from the culture group (57 percent), followed by the science group (40 percent).

The public, for its part, once again disagrees with the influentials, and wants a vastly diminished role for America in the future. Average citizens voiced almost as much support for America's playing no leadership role at all as for its being the world's single leader (seven and ten percent, respectively).[11]

Among those who support a shared leadership role (81 percent), the public, by a two-to-one margin, wanted the United States to be neither more nor less active than other leading nations.[12] This is essentially the reverse of the influentials' overwhelming preference for the more assertive role.

Trend data from earlier surveys indicate the same broad inclination toward isolationism among the public over the past three decades.[13] Asked if the United States should go its own way in international matters, 34 percent said yes this year, up steadily from 19 percent in 1964 (figure 4). Asked if the United States should concentrate more on its own national problems rather than think so much in international terms, 78 percent agreed this year, up from 55 percent in 1964 (figure 5). Asked if the United States should mind its own business internationally and let other coun-

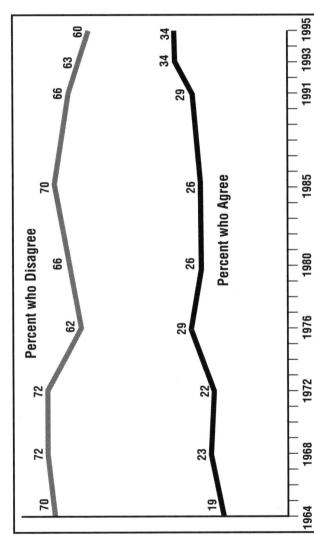

FIGURE 4. "SINCE THE U.S. IS THE MOST POWERFUL NATION IN THE WORLD, WE SHOULD GO OUR OWN WAY IN INTERNATIONAL MATTERS, NOT WORRYING TOO MUCH ABOUT WHETHER OTHER COUNTRIES AGREE WITH US OR NOT."

Source: Times Mirror Center for the People and the Press, *Public Opinion of the U.N.: Strong Support, Strong Criticism* (Washington, D.C.: Times Mirror Center for the People and the Press, 1995).

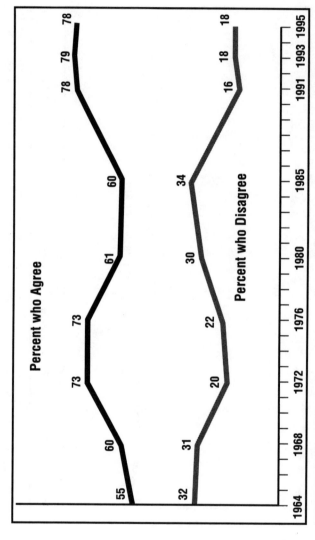

FIGURE 5. "WE SHOULD NOT THINK SO MUCH IN INTERNATIONAL TERMS BUT CONCENTRATE MORE ON OUR OWN NATIONAL PROBLEMS AND BUILDING UP OUR STRENGTH AND PROSPERITY HERE AT HOME."

Sources: * All trend data are from public opinion surveys conducted by Potomac Associates, the Gallup Organization, and the Institute for International Social Research. The most recent figures from April 1993 and June 1995 are from surveys conducted by the Times Mirror Center.

tries get along as best they can, 41 percent said yes this year, compared with 18 percent in 1964 (figure 6). This last measure of disengagement—minding our own business—was higher in the immediate post-Vietnam period (41 percent in 1976); nonetheless, it has risen markedly over the last 30 years.

The one exception to the trend toward disengagement is some degree of support for the United Nations. Asked whether the United States should cooperate fully with the United Nations, 46 percent answered yes in 1976, while 71 percent said yes in 1993 (figure 7). The percentage of Americans who agree with this statement dropped to 62 percent in June 1995. However, the public is far from willing to put American troops under U.N. commanders (69 percent opposed, 25 percent in favor). In contrast, influentials were willing to do so in almost precisely the opposite proportion.

3. AMERICAN VALUES AND ATTITUDES

Since the late 1980s, there has been widespread discontent with the political system and the political status quo in the United States. In study after study, the Times Mirror Center has found that more Americans than ever feel that Washington leaders have lost touch with the people, that elected officials do not care about them, and that the government is not run in the people's best interest (see table 7). Jobs and the domestic economy are issues that surveys repeatedly show to be of paramount concern to citizens of all ages.

Times Mirror discovered during the 1992 presidential election that close to 85 percent of the public agreed that it was time for politicians to step aside and make room for new leaders. Agreement with this proposition increased by more than 20 points in just two years. Current public evaluations of President Bill Clinton's job performance reflect further public impatience with his political leadership. As table 8 demonstrates, Clinton's approval ratings are well below those of any president from Truman to Bush at a comparable point in time.

High levels of dissatisfaction with the country's leadership are most evident for the generation of Americans aged 50 and older, which does not confine its anger to elected officials. Older citizens are more likely than

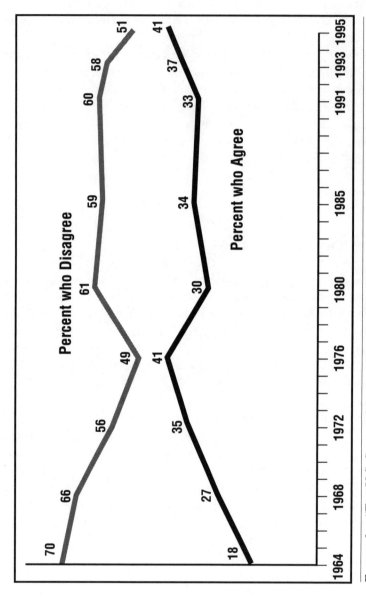

FIGURE 6. "THE U.S. SHOULD MIND ITS OWN BUSINESS INTERNATIONALLY AND LET OTHER COUNTRIES GET ALONG THE BEST WAY THEY CAN ON THEIR OWN."

Source: Times Mirror Center for the People and the Press, *Public Opinion of the U.N.*

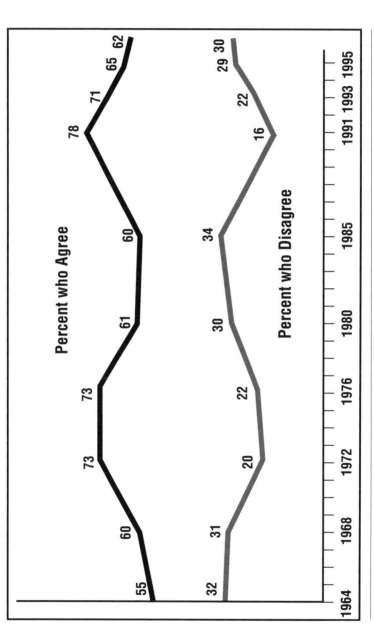

FIGURE 7. "THE UNITED STATES SHOULD COOPERATE FULLY WITH THE UNITED NATIONS"

Source: Times Mirror Center for the People and the Press, *Public Opinion of the U.N.*

TABLE 6. PERCENTAGE OF RESPONDENTS BY PREFERENCE FOR U.S. WORLD LEADERSHIP ROLE

| | Single World Leader | Shared Role | | None | Don't Know | (N) |
		Most Active	No More or Less Active Than Others			
News Media	9	62	22	3	4	(79)
Business/Finance	12	62	23	0	3	(69)
Cultural	5	37	57	0	1	(79)
Foreign Affairs	7	68	16	0	9	(69)
Defense/Security	17	58	17	0	8	(66)
State/Local Government	1	77	17	0	5	(69)
Think Tanks/Academics	7	60	25	0	8	(77)
Religion	4	53	38	0	5	(47)
Science/Engineering	7	48	40	2	3	(91)
General Public						
Sept. 1993	10	27	51	7	5	(2,000)
June 1995	13	25	47	9	6	(1,500)

Sources: Times Mirror Center for the People and the Press, America's Place in the World; and Public Opinion of the U.N.

TABLE 7. PERCENTAGE OF RESPONDENTS AGREEING WITH VARIOUS
STATEMENTS ABOUT GOVERNMENT AND ELECTED OFFICIALS, 1987–1994

	1987	1990	1991	1992	1993	1994
People like me don't have any say about what the government does.	52	57	50	50	52	54
Generally speaking, elected officials in Washington lose touch with the people pretty quickly.	73	78	84	84	82	83
Most elected officials care what people like me think.	47	44	63	63	63	3
The government is really run for the benefit of all the people.	57	52	48	44	—	42

Source: Times Mirror Center surveys.

TABLE 8. PERCENTAGE OF RESPONDENTS WHO APPROVE OF THE
PRESIDENT'S PERFORMANCE DURING THE FIRST TERM IN OFFICE

	%
Clinton (1993)	43
Bush (1989)	70
Reagan (1981)	60
Carter (1977)	66
Nixon (1969)	60

Sources: Clinton—Times Mirror Center; Truman through Reagan—Gallup Poll.
Note: Data are from surveys taken in September of the year indicated.

middle-aged people to rail against the inefficiencies of the federal bureaucracy. At the same time, they call into question the power and profits of big business. As table 9 demonstrates, people aged 50 and older voice more criticism of politics, business, and federal bureaucracy than do younger citizens.[14]

Still, no matter how critical Americans may be of political leaders or the way the process works, they have always maintained high levels of support for their system of government and political institutions. There is

TABLE 9. PERCENTAGE OF RESPONDENTS WHO COMPLETELY AGREE WITH VARIOUS VIEWS OF THE FEDERAL GOVERNMENT AND BUSINESS, BY AGE GROUP

	18–34	35–49	50+
Bureaucracy			
When something is run by the government, it is usually inefficient and wasteful			
May 1993	26	29	38
July 1994	27	36	38
The federal government controls too much of our daily lives			
May 1993	28	32	40
July 1994	32	35	43
Business			
There is too much power concentrated in the hands of a few big companies			
May 1993	31	32	37
July 1994	30	31	33
Business corporations make too much profit			
May 1993	32	30	38
July 1994	22	19	25

Source: Times Mirror Center surveys.

perhaps no other question in polling history that receives such consistent and universal approval as the one that asks Americans if their system of government is the best in the world. Times Mirror has found that Americans generally have favorable attitudes toward political institutions, including local and state government, the courts, special interest groups, and the media. As table 10 indicates, Congress is the only government institution included in the survey that was seen as having a negative influence on the country by the American public.

Racial Tensions

Racial tensions in the United States have heightened in the aftermath of the Rodney King verdict and the April 1992 riots in Los Angeles. A large majority of Americans—77 percent of whites and 83 percent of blacks—admit that there is discrimination against blacks today. Further, there is

TABLE 10.   PERCENTAGE OF RESPONDENTS WHO BELIEVE THAT VARIOUS INSTITUTIONS ARE A GOOD INFLUENCE ON THE COUNTRY

	%
Congress	37
Supreme Court	73*
Courts	51
Local and state governments	60
Democratic Party	57*
Republican Party	54*
Police	69
Newspapers	72
Network TV news	81*
CNN	76
People who run their own businesses	91
Business executives	41
Environmentalists	75
Women's movement	68

Source: Times Mirror Center surveys, July 1992 and July 1993.
Note: *For 1993, responses reflect "very favorable" and "mostly favorable" evaluations of institutions.

widespread belief that blacks hold an inferior position in American society. In 1987 only 25 percent of whites agreed that the position of black people in the past few years had not improved. That percentage rose to 41 percent in 1991, reached 54 percent in 1992, and remained at 47 percent in 1993.[15]

The vast majority of whites—more than 60 percent—are opposed to preferential treatment of blacks and other minorities as a means of improving their position in this country.[16] Blacks and other minority groups, to a somewhat lesser extent, support preferential treatment. The belief that black people have not made progress in this country is strongly held among black citizens (80 percent). This figure is up significantly from 67 percent in 1987.[17] Trends in racial tolerance are displayed in table 11.

There are significant generational differences in racial attitudes in the United States among both whites and blacks. White Americans younger than 50 are more sensitive to the problems of black people than are older people. Young whites are more likely than older whites to admit that blacks have not made sufficient progress in society and that discrimination is common. The opposite trend holds for blacks. The older generation is most likely to believe that blacks have not improved their position in society and that racial discrimination is a problem.

No More Melting Pot

Closely tied to Americans' racial attitudes are their concerns about new immigrant groups entering the country. In 1991 nearly 1.8 million people arrived in the country legally; between two million and four million people entered illegally. The United States accepts more immigrants than all other industrialized nations combined.

With immigration rates escalating, the public is worried that the situation is out of control. The Times Mirror Center found that 65 percent of Americans felt that stopping the flood of illegal aliens should be a top priority of the U.S. government.[18]

Citizens fear for their jobs, especially in areas of high unemployment, such as California and Texas. Relatedly, they are concerned that immigrants will place a heavy burden on public assistance programs, the criminal justice system, the health care system, and educational institutions. A Times Mirror poll revealed that 76 percent of Americans completely agree

TABLE 11. PERCENTAGE OF RESPONDENTS WHO AGREE WITH VARIOUS STATEMENTS ABOUT RACIAL ISSUES, 1987–1994

	1987	1991	1992	1993	1994
Whites					
In the past few years there hasn't been much real improvement in the position of black people in this country	25	41	54	47	44
We should make every possible effort to improve the position of blacks and other minorities even if it means giving them preferential treatment	25	26	29	28	25
Discrimination against blacks is rare today	—	—	19	—	23
I think it's alright for blacks and whites to date each other	56	63	61	—	65
Blacks					
In the past few years there hasn't been much real improvement in the position of black people in this country	67	73	82	80	73
We should make every possible effort to improve the position of blacks and other minorities even if it means giving them preferential treatment	62	60	67	60	62
Discrimination against blacks is rare today	—	—	15	—	26
I think it's alright for blacks and whites to date each other	84	86	81	—	88

Source: Times Mirror Center surveys.

with the statement that the United States should restrict and control people immigrating here more than we do now.[19] A 1993 *Newsweek* survey revealed that 60 percent of Americans feel that immigration is bad for the country, although 59 percent believe that immigration in the past was good.[20] A majority of those surveyed (59 percent) presume that many immigrants end up on welfare.

Worried about their own safety and economic security, Americans are unwilling to make it easier for any immigrant group to settle in this country, including East Europeans. They even favor elimination of education, health, and welfare benefits for illegal immigrants and their children (53 percent in favor versus 41 percent opposed in a December 1994 Times Mirror Center survey). They advocate making it more difficult for Middle Easterners, Haitians, Asians, Latin Americans, and Africans, in particular, to immigrate. A strong majority of respondents to the *Newsweek* survey contend that immigrants do not make an effort to assimilate American culture and values. Instead, 66 percent believe that most immigrants maintain their own national identity, and that the idea of America as a "melting pot" has become a myth.

Social Responsibility versus Self-Reliance

As attitudes toward race have shifted in recent years, attitudes on social justice and self-reliance also appear to have changed dramatically. While nine out of ten Americans still agree that our society should do what is necessary to make sure everyone has an equal opportunity to succeed, there has been a significant decline in support for social welfare programs.

In a 1994 survey by Times Mirror, 57 percent of the public agreed it is the responsibility of the government to take care of people who cannot take care of themselves—down from 69 percent in 1992 and 71 percent in 1987 (see table 12). Only 41 percent believed that the government should help more needy people even if it means going deeper in debt (compared with 56 percent who disagreed). This is the first time that this premise has not received majority support in Times Mirror surveys; in both 1987 and 1992, for example, 53 percent agreed.

Personal Freedom, Tolerance, and Moral Values

Although their society prides itself on its constitutionally guaranteed protection of individual freedoms, Americans historically have been divided

TABLE 12. PERCENTAGE OF RESPONDENTS WHO AGREE WITH VARIOUS
STATEMENTS ABOUT WELFARE 1987–94

	1987	1990	1991	1992	1993	1994
Our society should do what is necessary to make sure that everyone has an equal opportunity to succeed	90	91	94	93	—	91
The government should help more needy people even if it means going deeper into debt	53	51	51	53	43	41
The government should guarantee every citizen enough to eat and a place to sleep	62	62	73	66	—	59
We have gone too far in pushing equal rights in this country	42	43	38	40	43	48
It is the responsibility of the government to take care of people who can't take care of themselves	71	67	—	69	62	57

Source: Times Mirror Center surveys.

on tolerance issues. Studies dating back to the 1950s demonstrated that the public was unwilling to grant basic freedom of speech and assembly to communists. Since the end of the Cold War, the public has been more accepting of communists, but still has problems applying the norms of political tolerance universally.

AIDS has made homosexuals a greater target for intolerance. Thirty-nine percent of the public feel that school boards have the right to fire teachers who are homosexuals. Almost as many people believe that AIDS might be God's punishment for immoral sexual behavior. A more generalized attitude of intolerance is reflected in the fact that almost 51 percent of the public believe that books that contain dangerous ideas should be banned from public school libraries.[21]

Again, the generation aged 50 and older sets itself apart from younger people by being far less tolerant. Among people younger than 35, 67 percent disapprove of homosexuals' being fired by school boards, compared with 42 percent of Americans aged 50 and older. A strong majority of older people (61 percent) support banning books with dangerous ideas, while only 40 percent of the under-30 generation agree with this policy.[22]

An Energized Public

Disillusionment with the economy and political leadership has translated into political action in the United States. The 20-year downward spiral in turnout was broken as 61 percent of the electorate voted in 1992, an increase of four percentage points from the previous election. (Turnout data for the past eight elections are presented in table 13.) People were also more interested in issues, as opposed to personalities, in 1992 than in past contests. Further, outsider and presidential candidate Ross Perot launched

TABLE 13.   PERCENTAGE OF THE ELECTORATES VOTING IN
PRESIDENTIAL ELECTIONS, 1964–92, BY AGE

	1992	1988	1984	1980	1976	1972	1968	1964
Total	61	57	60	59	59	63	68	69
18–24	43	36	41	40	42	49	50	51
25–44	58	54	58	59	59	63	67	69
45–64	70	68	70	69	69	71	75	76
65+	70	69	68	65	62	64	66	66

Source: U.S. Department of Commerce, Economics and Statistics Administration, Bureau of the Census, "Voting and Registration in the Election," *Current Population Reports,* pp. 20–466.

the first meaningful third-party candidacy in decades, buoyed by a flurry of grass-roots support unmatched in recent history.

In dramatic contrast to past eras of social and political transition when young people led the way, the vanguard of the movement toward political change in America is composed of older Americans. It is citizens over 50 who are most unhappy with the political system and who call most vigorously for a change in political leadership. Older voters were the first to be attracted to Ross Perot, and their enthusiasm for Perot is unmatched by any other generational cohort. Nearly two out of three older Americans take the position that new leadership is needed, even if there is a chance it will be ineffective. Fewer than half of those under 30 favor following this course.[23]

At the same time the older generation is expressing its discontent, the Baby Boomers—the generation of people in their mid-thirties and forties—also has assumed a larger role in the political process. Bill Clinton is the first Baby Boomer president of the United States, and his leadership style and worldview, if not all of his policy pronouncements, reflect the activist roots of this generation. Baby Boomers give cautious support to the president's reform policies, which are in keeping with the credos of their youth, but which are somewhat at odds with the high socioeconomic status they have achieved in society.

In dramatic contrast to the overall movement toward an activist public, younger citizens show no major inclination toward becoming vigorous political participants. Politically, Americans under 35 years of age are far more apathetic than their Baby Boomer predecessors or the newly activated members of the over-50 generation. They are not interested in politics, they lack political knowledge, and they have poor voting records. However, they are not as critical of government as young people have been in the past. Nor do they express as many reservations about political institutions, government bureaucracy, and business as older citizens. Interestingly, the Americans younger than 30 show more benevolent attitudes toward institutions and leaders than their older counterparts because they are simply ambivalent about them, not because they have less with which to find fault. Surprisingly, as table 13 demonstrates, voter turnout increased more among this generation than among older people, as President Bill Clinton reached out to young people through unconventional forums, such as MTV.

4. THE INFORMATION REVOLUTION

As Americans have become increasingly discontented with their leaders and the domestic scene, they have acquired an ever-increasing array of mass media options that not only inundate them with political news, but also allow them to vent their displeasure. New technologies, such as cable television and computer networks, have made a substantial mark on the information scene. Old media, such as talk radio, are assuming fresh identities and gaining new audiences. Entertainment media, such as television talk shows and tabloid magazines, provide alternative outlets for political expression. The Times Mirror Center has monitored the public's use of different types of media and has documented the changes in mass communication that have evolved in recent years. Our survey data support several conclusions about how the information revolution has altered the public's relationship to mass media institutions, politics, and culture.

The Emergence of Mass Media Populism

One noteworthy development is the degree to which politics has evolved into a new form of mass entertainment, resulting in a kind of media populism that is unprecedented in American history. During the 1992 presidential election campaign, candidates departed from the traditional strategy of hard news management and made appeals through popular media channels, including talk radio, MTV, and late-night talk shows. The trend took hold, and "infotainment" politics—the combination of politics with entertainment fare—has become entrenched in the American mass media system. Political information in its many guises now saturates media markets targeting people from all segments of society, not just those occupying the upper rungs of the socioeconomic ladder.

Further, the dynamics of the mass media's relationship to the citizenry have changed markedly. Not so long ago, the media engaged primarily in reporting news to an essentially passive public and presenting the views of elites. Now, new forums, such as electronic town meetings, provide opportunities for average citizens to participate publicly in political dialogue. Computer networks make political leaders seem accessible to the public to a degree previously never dreamed possible. Americans communicate so often with President Clinton by electronic mail via computer that his on-line mailboxes are frequently filled to capacity with messages, all of which are answered, and some of which are actually read by top White House officials.[24] Thus, under the new system of media populism, the mass public's role has been transformed from that of a spectator to an actor in the constantly unfolding drama of politics.

A Times Mirror Center study released in July 1993 entitled *The Vocal Minority in American Politics* explored the implications of these fresh developments in political communication and activity, including talk radio, phone-in television programs, and call-in opinion polls.[25] The study revealed that these newly emergent channels of public opinion enjoy high levels of popularity. For example, our nationwide survey disclosed that almost one-half of all Americans listen to talk radio on a relatively frequent basis, with one in six tuning in regularly. The poll also indicates that while talk radio attracts millions of listeners, millions of people either have expressed or aspire to express their opinions on the air.

The new channels of media populism are used primarily to vent disapproval of political institutions and leaders, especially government insiders. Republican voices resonate more loudly than those of Democrats, and conservative positions on issues are overrepresented. Correspondingly, this vocal minority is much more critical of President Clinton and his policies than is the average American. Clinton's disapproval rating is 10 to 15 percentage points higher among people who have talked on the radio, written their congressional representative, or responded to call-in polls than it is among the general population.

New versus Old Media

It is important at this stage, however, not to overestimate the power or significance of these new media. Newer information formats have not dislodged the mainstream press from its position at the top of the media/information hierarchy. The role played by traditional political media, such as newspapers and network television news, has been marginally influenced by popular media. The effects are seen primarily in terms of what traditional media feel compelled to cover, rather than how it is covered. The mainstream press finds itself in the awkward position of reporting news events staged for alternative media, while at the same time decrying the affront to journalistic standards that "showbizification

of politics"—to use a term coined by CBS News anchor Dan Rather—
represents.

The most direct challenge to print and broadcast news comes not
from the populist media formats, but from CNN, C-Span, and other man-
ifestations of real-time news. Newspapers and the major television networks cannot win the competition to be first with breaking stories when
the public has 24-hour-a-day access to all-news channels. This point is
best illustrated by the results of a Times Mirror survey conducted in March
1991, which revealed that more people identified CNN as the network
doing the best job of covering the war in the Persian Gulf than named the
three broadcast networks combined.

The changes brought about by the information revolution seem to
have the worst effect on television network news, rather than newspapers.
Nightly newscasts cannot keep up with the all-news channels in presenting up-to-the-minute reports, provide the depth and perspective of print
media, or be as dynamic and engaging as talk radio shows. In an environment in which all news stations furnish the headlines, and call-in programs supply the excitement, newspapers can fill in the details and provide
analysis much more effectively than can broadcast television.

In spite of these trends, none of the newer forms of political media—
neither CNN nor radio nor television call-in programs—come close to the
popularity of the old standbys, including network news. As table 14 reveals
in 1993, a far higher proportion of people regularly read their daily newspaper (66 percent) and watched nightly national (60 percent) or local television
news broadcasts (77 percent) than monitored any other form of mass media.[26]

Further, as table 15 demonstrates, our respondents report that they
learn more about politics from mainstream sources than from any alternative outlet. More than 40 percent of Americans claimed that they learned
a great deal about the Clinton administration from their daily newspapers, news magazines, such as *Time* and *Newsweek*, and nightly network
news broadcasts. Far fewer could say the same about any other source,
including CNN (36 percent, although CNN is available only to approximately half of our respondents).

Alternative media do not cut into the audience for traditional print
and broadcast offerings. Rather, people who attend to new sources of
political information tend to be heavy consumers of newspapers and
nightly television news. A few examples highlight the general pattern that

TABLE 14.   PERCENTAGE OF RESPONDENTS WHO REGULARLY ATTEND
TO SPECIFIC TYPES OF MASS MEDIA

	May 1993	1994/1995
PRINT MEDIA		
Read daily newspaper	66	—
Read news magazines, such as *Time,*		
U.S. *News and World Report,*		
or *Newsweek*	24	18
TELEVISION		
Watch the national nightly network news		
on CBS, ABC, or NBC	60	48†
Watch local news about their viewing area	77	72†
Watch Cable News Network (CNN)	35	30†
Watch C-Span	11	8†
Watch TV news magazine shows, such as "60		
Minutes" or "20/20"	52	43*
Watch Sunday morning news shows, such		
as "Meet the Press," "Face the Nation," or		
"This Week with David Brinkley"	18	—
Watch "MacNeil Lehrer NewsHour"	10	7*
Watch the "Larry King" show	5	—
RADIO		
Listen to programs on National Public		
Radio, such as "Morning Edition" or "All		
Things Considered"	15	15†
Listen to talk radio shows that invite		
listeners to call in to discuss current		
events, public issues, and politics	17	12†
Listen to Rush Limbaugh's radio show	—	6*
ENTERTAINMENT MEDIA		
Watch television talk shows, such as "Oprah,"		
"Donahue," or "Geraldo"	24	—
Read personality magazines, such as *People*		
or *US*	12	9‡

Source: Times Mirror Center surveys.
*July 1994.
†March 1995.
‡February 1994.

TABLE 15. PERCENTAGE OF RESPONDENTS WHO REPORT
LEARNING A GREAT DEAL ABOUT THE CLINTON ADMINISTRATION
FROM SPECIFIC TYPES OF MASS MEDIA

PRINT MEDIA	
Daily newspaper	43
News magazines, such as *Time, U.S. News and World Report,* or *Newsweek*	45
TELEVISION	
National nightly network news on CBS, ABC, or NBC	45
Local news about their viewing area	38
Cable News Network (CNN)	36
C-Span	14
TV news magazine shows, such as "60 Minutes" or "20/20"	30
Sunday morning news shows, such as "Meet the Press," "Face the Nation," or "This Week with David Brinkley"	19
"MacNeil/Lehrer News Hour"	12
The "Larry King" show	7
RADIO	
Programs on National Public Radio, such as "Morning Edition" or "All Things Considered"	12
Talk radio shows that invite listeners to call in to discuss current events, public issues, and politics	18
ENTERTAINMENT MEDIA	
Television talk shows, such as "Oprah," "Donahue," or "Geraldo"	12
Personality magazines, such as *People* or *US*	6

Source: Times Mirror Center for the People and the Press, *The Vocal Minority in American Politics* (Washington, D.C.: Times Mirror Center for the People and the Press, 1993).

appears in table 16. While 77 percent of those who watch CNN frequently also routinely read the newspaper, 74 percent regularly watch television network news. Of habitual talk radio listeners, 72 percent are regular newspaper readers and 68 percent watch the nightly news often. Readers of personality magazines are voracious newspaper readers (81 percent) and spend a good deal of time viewing nightly news programs (69 percent).

TABLE 16. PERCENTAGE OF RESPONDENTS WHO REGULARLY
ATTEND TO VARIOUS MASS MEDIA AND WHO READ NEWSPAPERS
OR WATCH TV NEWS

Regularly attend to:	Read Newspaper	Watch TV News
PRINT MEDIA		
Daily newspaper	—	66
News magazines, such as *Time, U.S. News and World Report*, or *Newsweek*	85	77
TELEVISION		
National nightly network news on CBS, ABC, or NBC.	74	—
Local news about your viewing area	72	73
Cable News Network (CNN)	77	75
C-Span	75	75
TV news magazine shows, such as "60 Minutes" or "20/20"	73	76
Sunday morning news shows, such as "Meet the Press," "Face the Nation," or "This Week with David Brinkley"	81	84
"MacNeil/Lehrer NewsHour"	83	72
The "Larry King" show	79	78
RADIO		
Programs on National Public Radio, such as "Morning Edition" or "All Things Considered"	75	72
Talk radio shows that invite listeners to call in to discuss current events, public issues, and politics	72	68
ENTERTAINMENT MEDIA		
Television talk shows, such as "Oprah," "Donahue," or "Geraldo"	66	66
Personality magazines, such as *People* or *US*	81	69

Source: Times Mirror Center for the People and the Press, *The Vocal Minority in American Politics.*

There is also substantial overlap in the audience for newspapers and television news, which has important implications. Three-fourths of the respondents in our study who regularly read a newspaper also regularly watch network television news. These people, comprising 45 percent of our total sample, come disproportionately from the most affluent, best-educated segments of society. Among college graduates, 46 percent regularly attend to both newspapers and television. Only 11 percent of those with a high school diploma or less are so oriented. The pattern follows similar lines for income, as 48 percent of those surveyed who earn more than $50,000 per year regularly use both media, compared with 28 percent of those earning $20,000 or less.

5. SOME FURTHER IMPLICATIONS

The lack of consensus among U.S. elites about America's place in the new world order suggests that in the future they may lead the public on foreign policy issues less than they did in the Cold War era. The rallying appeal of anticommunism facilitated a leader-follower relationship not likely to be matched in the current environment.

Other factors may well increase in importance. For example, some would contend that the advent of real-time news broadcasts is giving the public more of an opportunity to form its own conclusions about international issues. The broad array of media outlets that enables those interested to watch rebroadcasts of House of Commons debates or Russian newscasts may well create high levels of information about international issues among microsegments of the public.

Populist leaders and media outlets that have fueled public anger about government policies and actions may have a louder voice in the future on international issues. A population that has become focused inward is vulnerable to such influences. The foreign policy points of view fostered in this environment would likely be less international and more parochial in vision. The public's lack of awareness of international issues growing out of its indifference can only facilitate such results.

In that connection, the generation that is poised to assume leadership roles in the 21st century has demonstrated a stunning lack of attention to international affairs. The interests of Americans younger than 35 have been more narrowly focused. Unlike previous generations, this age cohort's political experience so far has not been shaped by a major international conflict. These factors will raise significant questions about the disposition of this generation as it moves to a position of authority in years to come.

More optimistically, considerable evidence suggests that there is an opportunity for America's leadership to rally public support behind U.S. efforts addressing issues that have been identified as of domestic concern, but that transcend national borders. Such efforts could, in fact, become the basis for new transatlantic cooperation between the United States and those west European nations whose publics are sympathetically concerned with similar issues. Many come quickly to mind.

Certain to attract support among publics on both sides of the Atlantic, for example, would be any initiatives seeking not only to halt proliferation of nuclear weapons and fissionable weapons material, but also to reduce the danger of accidents at nuclear power-generating stations (like Chernobyl) and weapons storage sites. International programs to find suitable sites for nuclear waste disposal would also find wide support with the American public. Similarly, programs to curb the international epidemics of crime, drug abuse, AIDS, illegal immigration, and regional and global ecological pollution would be welcomed by publics on both continents.

Finally, but not least among such potential programs, would be joint, military-led humanitarian efforts at famine relief and peacekeeping (but not peacemaking) in regions of tribal slaughter (Rwanda) and ethnic or religious conflict (Bosnia).

NOTES

1. Andrew Kohut and Robert C. Toth, *America's Place in the New World,* (Washington, D.C.: Times Mirror Center for the People and the Press, 1993).
2. The Times Mirror Influential Americans Survey, conducted during the summer of 1993, obtained completed interviews with 649 individuals. The accompanying telephone interview survey of the general public consisted of a nationwide sample of 2,000 adults, 18 years of age or older, conducted between September 9 and September 15, 1993. After weighing, this sample forms a demographically representative cross-section of American society. For results based on the entire sample, the sampling error is plus or minus two percentage points. (For more detailed information about these studies see Kohut and Toth, *America's Place in the World.*)

3. More recent surveys by Times Mirror indicate the public continues to be dissatisfied with the way things are going in the country—73 percent expressed this sentiment in both July 1994 and June 1995.
4. American public opinion has not changed in the two years since the original study was conducted, as evidenced by identical findings in a Times Mirror survey from June 1995. A majority continue to identify protection of American jobs as the top foreign policy goal (80 percent), followed again by nuclear proliferation concerns (68 percent), ensuring adequate energy supplies (59 percent), and protection of the environment (56 percent).
5. A more recent example of the public's opposition to promotion of democracy abroad is that in an August 1995 Times Mirror survey, fully two-thirds believe the United States should not get involved in China's domestic affairs, even at the risk of overlooking human rights abuses.
6. Americans are also opposed to the use of U.S. military force in Bosnia to help end the fighting there (61 percent versus 32 percent favor), unless U.N. peacekeepers come under attack (71 percent favor versus 22 percent oppose), or to help U.N. peacekeepers move to safer places (65 percent favor versus 29 percent oppose). See Time Mirror Center survey, June 1995.
7. In February 1995, the Times Mirror Center found greater percentages saying defense spending should be kept the same (56 percent) or increased (19 percent), and a smaller percentage saying it should be cut back (24 percent, down from 36 percent in 1993).
8. Andrew Kohut, Robert C. Toth, and Carol Bowman, *Cautious Support for Clinton Plan* (Washington, D.C.: Times Mirror Center for the People and the Press, 1993).
9. Support for NAFTA peaked at the end of 1993, when 52 percent said they favored the free trade agreement, but it dropped back to 43 percent in March 1995. However, in July 1994, 62 percent of the public said they favor free trade agreements such as NAFTA and the General Agreement on Tariffs and Trade. See Times Mirror Center survey, July 1994.
10. And more than a year later, an even greater percentage of Americans said the United States is playing a *more* important role as world leader (40 percent in December 1994).
11. Again, there has been relatively little change in the public's view on this issue; only 13 percent in June 1995 said the United States should be the single world leader, and 74 percent opted for a shared leadership role.
12. A similar margin was found in June 1995; 47 percent said the United States should be no more or less active and 25 percent said it should be the most active.
13. All trend data are from public opinion surveys conducted by Potomac Associates, the Gallup Organization, and the Institute for International Social Research. Figures for April 1993 through June 1995 are from surveys conducted by the Times Mirror Center.

14. More recent survey results show similar feelings toward the government by the different age groups, but there is much less of a generation gap on attitudes toward the power of big business in 1994, and there has been a significant decline among all age groups in the belief that businesses make too much profit.
15. A Times Mirror Center poll in July 1994 indicates that a large majority of Americans—74 percent of both whites and blacks—continue to believe there is discrimination against blacks; and the percentage of white Americans who agree that the position of black people has not improved has declined to 44 percent.
16. This percentage increased to 73 percent in July 1994.
17. The percentage of black Americans who said they agreed with this view in July 1994 had declined to 73 percent.
18. As recently as June 1995, 61 percent of the public still views this as a top priority, preceded only by concerns about international drug trafficking and strengthening of the domestic economy.
19. Donald Kellermann, Andrew Kohut, and Carol Bowman, *The Generations Divide* (Washington, D.C.: Times Mirror Center for the People and the Press, 1992).
20. Tom Morganthau, "America: Still a Melting Pot," *Newsweek*, August 9, 1993, pp. 16–25.
21. These numbers have remained essentially unchanged. As recently as July 1994, 39 percent of the public said school boards have the right to fire homosexual teachers; an equal percentage believed AIDS might be God's punishment for immoral sexual behavior; and 51 percent believed that books with dangerous ideas ought to be banned from public school libraries.
22. Again, July 1994 figures indicate very little shift: 70 percent of those under 35 and 44 percent of those aged 50 and older disapproved of firing homosexual teachers; and, 64 percent of the oldest respondents and 44 percent of those under 30 supported book banning.
23. Figures for 1994 indicate this generation gap is narrowing; 64 percent of those over 50 believe new leadership is needed, as do 56 percent of those under 30 years of age.
24. "A Note to Bill: Writing the White House," *PC World*, October 1993, pp. 229–30.
25. Andrew Kohut, Cliff Zukin, and Carol Bowman, *The Vocal Minority in American Politics* (Washington, D.C.: Times Mirror Center for the People and the Press, 1993).
26. More recent Times Mirror Center surveys show a decline in the percentage of the public who say they "regularly" attend to any of these media behaviors, as the table shows.

INDEX

spending cuts favored by influentials, 78–79
troops deployed abroad, 77–78
troop strength in Europe, 79
troop strength in South Korea, 79
Democracies, Western pluralist, 58–59
Democracy
effect on Cold War, 1
dissatisfaction with, 58
promotion (as U.S. foreign policy
goal), 74
West European satisfaction with
(figure), 40
breakdown in Western Europe,
39–42
Denmark, support for European unification in (figure), 45
Diminishing marginal utility, law of,
24
Dutschke, Rudi, 33

Easton, David, 39
Ecology movements, 21
Economic growth rate versus age dif-
ferences (figure), 25
Economic well-being, continuation of,
21–22
Education, rise of, 4
student participation in Western
Europe (figure), 7
Elites, consensus about security in
OECD countries, 59–60
role of in forming new transna-
tional states, 42
Employment, change between 1970
and 1980, 3, 4–5
Energy, adequate supply of (as U.S.
foreign policy goal), 74
Environment (concern for in OECD
countries), 10
Environmental protection, global (as
U.S. foreign policy goal), 74
Ethnic groups, self-determination of,
76

Ethnic hatred, as threat to world stability, 71
Eurobarometer studies, advantage and
disadvantage of, 12
Europe
importance to United States, 79–80
planned U.S. troop strength in, 79
European Community, as U.S. trading
partner, 81
European integration. *See* European
unification.
European Science Foundation, 12
European states, factors affecting so-
ciopolitical orientations of, 58
European unification
attitudes toward, 42–43, 60
citizens' awareness of, 53
support for, 43–50, 53
support for by country, 45–50
Belgium (figure), 45
Denmark (figure), 45
France (figure), 47
Germany (figure), 46
Great Britain (figure), 50
Greece (figure), 46
Ireland (figure), 48
Italy (figure), 48
Luxembourg (figure), 49
Netherlands (figure), 49
Portugal (figure), 50
Spain (figure), 47
See also European Union
European Union
general attitudes toward, 42–53, 60
and creation of European Central
Bank, 51
and issue of common European cur-
rency, 51
Danish and British support for, 42
dissatisfaction with democracy in,
41–42
growth of, 58
effect of Maastricht Treaty on, 51
decreasing support for, 51

About the Authors

Max Kaase became research professor for the Comparative Study of Democracies Project at the Social Science Research Center in Berlin in October 1993. He has widely written and lectured on electoral research, political sociology, comparative politics, and the mass media. Since 1964 he has taught at the University of Mannheim as teaching assistant, assistant professor, adjunct lecturer, and extracurricular professor. He became full professor of political science in 1980. From 1974 to 1979 he was executive director of ZUMA, the center for polling, methods, and analysis in Mannheim.

Max Kaase is the author and editor of many books and articles. He co-edited with Hans-Dieter Klingemann *Wahlen und Wähler—Analysen aus Anlaß der Bundestagswahl 1990* (1994). His most recent book, *Beliefs in Government* (1995), was co-authored with Kenneth Newton. His recently published articles include "Is There Really Personalization in Politics? Candidates and Voting Behavior in Germany in Dynamic Perspective" (*International Political Science Review*, 1994) and "Electoral Research in the Federal Republic of Germany" (co-authored with Hans-Dieter Klingemann in *European Journal of Political Research*, 1994).

Andrew Kohut is director of the Times Mirror Center for the People & The Press in Washington D.C.

Kohut was president of The Gallop Organization from 1979 to 1989. In 1989 he founded Princeton Survey Research Associates, an attitude and opinion research firm specializing in media, politics, and public policy studies. He served as founding director of surveys for the Times Center 1990–92, and was named its director in 1993.

Kohut is a frequent press commentator on the meaning and interpretation of opinion poll results. In recent national elections he has served as a public opinion consultant and analyst for National Public Radio. He has also acted in that capacity for CNN, local broadcasting networks, and Fox News. Co-author of *The People, The Press and Politics* (1988), Kohut also has written widely about public opinion for leading newspapers and magazines, as well as for scholarly journals.

Kohut was president of the American Association of Public Opinion Research (1994–95). He is a trustee of the National Council on Public Polls and a member of the Market Research Council.

Kohut received an A.B. degree from Seton Hall University in 1964 and studied graduate sociology at Rutgers University.

The Project on the Future of the Transatlantic Relationship

The project represents a comprehensive research initiative on the future of the relationship between Europe and the United States. The demise of the East-West conflict raises questions about the durability of the transatlantic partnership. The security bonds across the Atlantic are becoming brittle. The relationship is beginning to show signs of strain and destabilization. The post–Cold War era calls for a new kind of active and creative cooperation across the Atlantic. Americans and Europeans must base their partnership on a new, positive definition.

Against this background, the Bertelsmann Foundation decided to carry out a research project on the future of the transatlantic relationship in concert with the Research Group on European Affairs at the University of Munich and the Council on Foreign Relations in New York. The project aims to produce policy-oriented proposals for shaping the future relationship between the United States and Europe, thus contributing to three crucial objectives: redirecting transatlantic cooperation toward the realities and requirements of the new international situation, stimulating economic and social innovation on both sides, and promoting international stability.

At the center of the project is an interdisciplinary Strategy Group of about 30 members, made up of established experts from both sides of the Atlantic. The project also engages a new generation of leading intellectuals in the form of Working Groups. Both the Strategy Group and the Working Groups meet on a regular basis, alternating between locations in Europe and America. Discussions are conducted on the basis of studies and shorter papers prepared by group members, their associate institutions, and outside experts. These analytical efforts result in concrete policy proposals that are circulated in the policy community. The project is also producing a book series, of which this volume is a part, to be published in both the United States and Europe.

The Project Partners

The Bertelsmann Foundation is committed to promoting innovation, generating ideas, injecting important issues into a broadly based debate, and, above all, helping to bring pressing problems closer to a solution. To accompany the process of political decision-making, the Bertelsmann Foundation, the Research Group on European Affairs at Munich University and the Council on Foreign Relations launched in 1993 a project on "The Future of the Transatlantic Relationship." The goal of this project is to offer practical solutions to urgent political problems and to participate in formulating long-term strategies.

The Research Group on European Affairs is part of the Geschwister-Scholl-Institute for Political Science at the Ludwig-Maximilians-University in Munich. The Research Group is now integrated into the new Center for Applied Policy Research—CAP—and can look back on more than ten years of intensive research into European issues. The Research Group possesses comprehensive research and publication faciliities. These include editorial teams, a research library, and the European Documentation Center, which has all the documents issued by the European Community institutions on file. It also has access to the European database network. The Research Group organizes various ongoing research projects, publications series, conferences, and symposiums.

The Council on Foreign Relations is a nonprofit and nonpartisan membership organization dedicated to improving the understanding of U.S. foreign policy through the exchange of ideas. The Council's principal activities, conducted in New York City, Washington, D.C., and elsewhere in the United States and abroad, are coordinated by its Meeting Program, Studies Program, Corporate Program, and various national outreach programs for members and the general public. Since 1922, the Council has published *Foreign Affairs*, the preeminent journal in the field.

The Council on Foreign Relations Press publishes books and occasional policy reports on a broad range of issues, which are made available to the public. The Council also produces "America and the World," a weekly radio series aired on National Public Radio and sponsors occasional televised policy hearings.